D1509340

| DATE DUE | | | |
|---|---|---|---|
| | | | |
| | | | |
| | | | |
| | | | |
| | | | |
| | | | |
| | | | |
| | | | |
| | | | |
| | | | |
| | | | |
| | | | |
| | | | |

# THE COLD WAR

# THE COLD WAR

BY MICHAEL G. KORT

THE MILLBROOK PRESS
BROOKFIELD, CONNECTICUT

17540

Library of Congress Cataloging-in-Publication Data
Kort, Michael, 1944–
The Cold War / by Michael G. Kort.
p.    cm.
Includes bibliographical references and index.
Summary: Covers the long ideological conflict between the
communist world and the Western democracies from the end of
World War II to the collapse of communism in Europe in 1990.
ISBN 1-56294-353-7
1. Cold War—Juvenile literature.    2. World politics—1945—
Juvenile literature.    [1. Cold War.    2. World politics.]
I. Title.
D843.K628    1994
909.82—dc20    93-1934    CIP    AC

Published by The Millbrook Press
2 Old New Milford Road, Brookfield, Connecticut 06804

For Uncle Heini
and in memory of Aunt Lilly

Photographs courtesy of UPI/Bettmann: pp. 13, 22, 42, 54, 56, 60, 61, 67, 72, 84, 90, 93, 99, 113, 125, 128, 147; AP/Wide World Photos: pp. 17, 37, 47, 77, 86, 110, 119, 133, 143, 150; National Archives: p. 27; LBJ Library: p. 116 (photo by Yoichi R. Okamoto); Reagan Library: p. 136.

# CONTENTS

# THE
# COLD
# WAR

# ONE

## THE BERLIN WALL
## AND THE COLD WAR

At 2:20 A.M. on Sunday, August 13, 1961, the silence of the night in Berlin, Germany, was suddenly shattered. The rumbling and clattering of hundreds of trucks and construction machines and the frantic activity of workmen and soldiers shook the center of the city. The soldiers occupied key points along a 25-mile (40-kilometer) line running through the center of the city, where the work was being done. Nobody was allowed to cross that line, except at a few closely guarded checkpoints. Laboring under the harsh glare of floodlights and cold stares of armed men, workers hurriedly tore up streets, threw up roadblocks, and rolled razor-sharp barbed wire into position. By daylight, a crude, unfinished barrier guarded by heavily armed soldiers and police stretched across much of the city, dividing Berlin into half. On the night of August 17–18, the construction of a high concrete wall began and what came to be called the Berlin Wall started to take shape.

The reason these workers were able to build a wall that divided the city is that in 1961 Berlin in reality was two cities: West and East Berlin. West Berlin belonged to the German Federal Republic, or West Germany, an ally of the United States. East Berlin was the capital of the German Democratic Republic, or East Germany, a Communist state dominated by the Soviet Union. Although West Berlin was surrounded by East German territory and 110 miles (175 kilometers) from West Germany, the city's residents were free to travel back and forth between West Berlin and West Germany. The soldiers and workmen who were building and guarding the Berlin Wall were East Germans, and the structure itself lay entirely in East Berlin. The wall was being built to prevent East Germans from fleeing their country by crossing over into West Berlin.

The Berlin Wall immediately became the single most familiar symbol of a great struggle of the mid- and late twentieth century known as the Cold War. The Cold War began in 1945 and lasted until 1990. It involved many nations, but the two main antagonists were the United States and the Union of Soviet Socialist Republics, or Soviet Union. In one sense the Cold War was a conventional power struggle between the two greatest military powers of the age. At its core, however, the Cold War was a struggle for world influence between two ways of life, each respectively most clearly represented by the United States and the Soviet Union. The United States was committed to political democracy and the capitalist economic system. The Soviet Union was a totalitarian dictatorship whose economy was based on Communist principles. The United States led an alliance of independent nations, while the Soviet Union dominated a bloc of Communist states.

Over the course of the struggle, each country armed itself to the teeth with thousands of nuclear weapons, enough to destroy the world many times over. So far did the United States and Soviet Union tower over all other

The concrete and barbed-wire barrier dividing West and
East Berlin became a symbol of Cold War tensions.

nations in military might that a new term—*superpower*—was coined to describe them. For decades the arms race between the superpowers kept the entire world under the threat of nuclear war. As their weapons became more destructive and each side developed guided missiles that traveled thousands of miles per hour, no more than thirty minutes separated any place in the world from nuclear destruction. Many of the world's intellectual leaders warned that civilization would be obliterated in a nuclear war. Thus in the 1950s Albert Einstein, the great genius whose theories form the foundation of modern physics, wrote that "unless we are able, in the near future, to abolish the fear of mutual aggression, we are doomed." In the 1960s, a well-known strategist named Herman Kahn predicted that "we are not going to reach the year 2000—and maybe not even the year 1965—without a cataclysm." And in the 1970s political scientist Hans Morgenthau warned that "the world is moving ineluctably towards a third world war—a strategic nuclear war."[1]

These concerns were not the nightmares of faint-hearted worrywarts. They were well grounded in reality, as the world learned during the Cuban Missile Crisis of 1962, when the Soviet Union and the United States came to the very brink of nuclear war and catastrophe.

In addition to building their nuclear might, each superpower sought allies and proxies wherever it could find them. Often this meant the United States supported dictatorships in various parts of the world whose policies most Americans would never have tolerated at home. For its part, the Soviet Union frequently helped non-Communist states who happened to be hostile to the United States for reasons having nothing to do with communism, democracy, or other issues that divided the superpowers.

1. Quoted in John Muller, "Quiet Cataclysm: Some Afterthoughts on World War III," in Michael J. Hogan, ed., *The End of the Cold War* (New York: Cambridge University Press, 1992), p. 43.

This immensely dangerous and intense struggle between the mightiest military powers of all time was called the Cold War—as opposed to a normal shooting, or "hot," war—because the two countries never directly fought each other. In fact, for the entire forty-five years of the Cold War the United States and Soviet Union legally were at peace. They had normal diplomatic relations, engaged in limited trade, competed in international sports events, and exchanged visits by cultural and artistic groups. Their leaders met in what were called "summit" meetings to try to improve relations and ease international tensions. The Cold War peace extended beyond the United States and Soviet Union to all of Europe. On that continent, where the Cold War began and ended, and where each superpower had its closest allies, no countries met on the battlefield while that long struggle raged.

Yet at the same time the United States and Soviet Union were bitterly hostile to each other. Each country viewed the other as aggressive by nature and a direct threat to its way of life. Because of their fears, both countries at times exaggerated the hostility of their opponent, endangering not only themselves but other nations caught in their great struggle. As Henry Kissinger, the U.S. secretary of state under Presidents Nixon and Ford, put it:

> The superpowers often behave like two heavily armed blind men feeling their way around a room, each believing himself in a mortal peril from the other whom he assumes to have perfect vision. . . . Of course, over time, even two blind men can do enormous danger to each other, not to speak of the room.[2]

The Cold War divided not only Berlin and Germany but also Europe and much of the rest of the world into two

2. Henry Kissinger, *The White House Years* (Boston: Little, Brown, 1979), p. 522.

hostile camps. Its battlegrounds, whether military, economic, or political, extended beyond Europe to Asia, Africa, and Latin America. There the Cold War was one cause of dozens of hot, or shooting, wars, large and small. Americans and Soviets did not kill each other in those conflicts, but nonetheless over 20 million people died. Among the more than thirty countries across the globe where violent struggle was made worse by the Cold War were Vietnam and Korea in Asia, Angola and Mozambique in Africa, and Nicaragua and El Salvador in Central America.

Although they never fought each other, the two superpowers did not escape unbloodied from the Cold War. The two largest hot spots of the Cold War for the United States were the Korean and the Vietnam wars. Between them they claimed almost 100,000 American lives and several million Korean and Vietnamese lives. The Korean War ended in a draw after three bitter years, leaving Americans deeply frustrated. The Vietnam War lasted almost three times as long and became the longest war in American history—and the only one the United States ever lost. The Soviet Union also fought a shooting war during the Cold War. In a brutal ten-year struggle in neighboring Afghanistan, approximately 15,000 Soviet soldiers and hundreds of thousands of Afghans lost their lives. And like the Americans in Vietnam, the Soviets were defeated in Afghanistan. The United States and Soviet Union shared something else in defeat: the local guerrilla forces that opposed them were backed and armed by the other superpower.

**U.S. tanks line up in a face-off against Soviet tanks in Berlin in 1961, during a dispute over access to the divided city. Despite such moments of high tension, the two countries never fought directly.**

The Cold War had other costs as well. The United States spent at least eight *trillion* dollars on its military while the Cold War raged. Because of this immense cost, many social needs—from education to health to basic transportation—were neglected for years. The Cold War also contributed greatly to an atmosphere of fear that gripped the United States in the early and mid-1950s. Many Americans were harassed because of their political beliefs and denied their basic constitutional rights. The Cold War also took its toll on the Soviet Union, which literally spent itself into collapse because it devoted so much of its wealth to its military. For almost half a century, the Cold War shaped the world in which we live.

The Berlin Wall therefore was a fitting symbol for the Cold War. Like the Cold War, it took on a life of its own. It grew to be 100 miles (160 kilometers) in length, surrounding the entire city of West Berlin. It became a sort of looming monster, complete with concrete watchtowers and floodlights for eyes, layers of barbed wire and electric fences for protective skin, and packs of heavily armed soldiers and vicious dogs for fangs. Like the Cold War itself, the Wall seemed to millions to be permanent and immovable, a constant reminder of the threat of nuclear war that lay behind an uneasy peace. And when the Berlin Wall was pierced in November 1989 and people were once again able to move freely about Berlin, a dagger had penetrated the heart of the Cold War. By mid-1990, the Cold War was dead.

How did the Cold War begin? Who was to blame for the failure to establish a genuine peace after World War II ended in 1945? What were the main crises and turning points of the Cold War? How and why did the Cold War finally end? These questions and others about this titanic struggle form the subject of this book.

## THE ORIGINS OF
## THE COLD WAR

Although the Cold War actually began just after World War II ended in 1945, some of its roots reach back as far as the nineteenth century. Russia, the giant among the countries of Europe, has long been feared by its smaller neighbors, at times even when they were allied with Russia against a common enemy. This fear cropped up immediately after Russia, Britain, and several other European nations defeated the French emperor Napoleon in 1812. The fighting had left Russia in an extremely powerful position in central Europe, which greatly worried not only England but other European powers as well. Russia's allies were so concerned that they threatened to join with France, their recently defeated enemy, against Russia unless Russia accepted limits on its power in central Europe. Not long afterward, in 1853, Britain, France, and several other European powers went to war with Russia to check its expansion in the Middle East. Britain, in fact, spent a great deal of its energy during the nineteenth century trying to limit Russian power. This British-Russian contest stretched across two continents, from the plains of central Europe to the mountains of Central Asia to the Pacific shores of the Far East.

By the early twentieth century, the United States also was concerned with Russia's power. Although the United States generally tried to stay out of European disputes, American leaders were concerned about any nation in Europe becoming too powerful. They worried that if any nation became powerful enough to dominate the European continent, it would be a threat to the well-being of the United States.

This was one reason why the United States in World War I supported Britain, France, and Russia against Germany. By World War I the Germans, as had the French under Napoleon, threatened to dominate Europe. This dangerous prospect helped convince America's leaders to go to war against Germany in 1917. But even as the United States opposed Germany, its leaders worried about Russia. As Colonel Edward House, one of President Woodrow Wilson's top advisers, put it, while it was essential to defeat Germany, an Allied victory presented serious problems of its own. An Allied victory, House worried, would lead "to the domination of Russia on the continent of Europe."[1]

In the midst of World War I a new element was added to the European and American fear of Russia. In November of 1917 a radical Marxist party called the Bolsheviks seized power in Russia, overthrowing a democratic government that had come to power only eight months earlier. The Bolsheviks believed in using violent revolution to

1. Quoted in Arthur S. Link, *Wilson: The Struggle for Neutrality, 1914–1915* (Princeton, N.J.: Princeton University Press, 1960), p. 48.

overthrow capitalism and establish socialism. As part of their plan to uproot capitalism in Russia and rebuild its society along socialist lines, they changed the country's name to the Union of Soviet Socialist Republics. In addition, the Bolsheviks made no secret of their desire to overthrow capitalism and democracy everywhere in the world. To the Bolsheviks, countries like Britain, France, and the United States were nothing but "imperialist" powers whose leaders used their industrial and military power to exploit their own working classes and take advantage of other nations. In 1919 the Bolshevik government founded an organization called the Communist International, or Comintern, whose job it was to spread the revolution to other countries. Vladimir Lenin, the leader of the Bolsheviks, made crystal clear what the Bolsheviks intended for the capitalist world:

> We live not only in a state, but in a system of states, and the existence of the Soviet Republic side by side with the imperialist states for a prolonged period of time is unthinkable. In the meantime a series of frightful collisions will occur.[2]

For its part, the United States strongly opposed the Bolshevik regime. The United States was angry that the Bolsheviks pulled Russia out of the war against Germany, and that it intended to spread its revolution to other countries. Between 1918 and 1920, the United States joined with the British and the French in an unsuccessful attempt to overthrow Bolshevism. Until 1933, the United States refused to recognize the Bolsheviks, who in 1918 changed their name to the Communist Party of the Soviet Union, as the legiti-

2. Quoted in G. H. Sterm, "The Foreign Policy of the Soviet Union," in F. S. Northedge, ed., *The Foreign Policies of the Great Powers* (New York: Praeger, 1962), p. 77.

Bolshevik leader Vladimir Lenin addresses a
crowd of his followers. Lenin believed that the
new Soviet state and the capitalist countries
of the West were on a collision course.

mate rulers of that country. And even after 1933, relations between the United States and the Soviet Union remained cool and suspicious at best.

## WORLD WAR II AND THE COLD WAR

World War II, which began in 1939, eventually brought the Soviet Union and the United States together in the struggle against Nazi Germany. However, the "Grand Alliance" against Germany, which included Great Britain and several other countries, was anything but grand. There was constant suspicion and friction between the Americans and British on the one hand and the Soviets on the other.

Some of these attitudes dated from the events already discussed, while others dated from the 1930s. The Soviets remembered the cowardly and disastrous Munich agreement the British and the French signed with Germany in 1938. In that agreement, in a desperate attempt to buy peace from Hitler, the British and the French allowed the German dictator to carve up the small country of Czechoslovakia. The Soviets, who had been willing to help Czechoslovakia, were excluded from the Munich talks. A year later, the Soviet leader, Joseph Stalin, had his revenge. He reached an agreement with Hitler in which the two countries promised not to attack each other. In addition, they secretly agreed to divide much of Eastern Europe between them. The agreement included the destruction of Poland, a country whose independence both Britain and France had promised to protect.

The Nazi-Soviet pact allowed Hitler to invade Poland and then to fight France and England without having to worry about the powerful Soviet Red Army. After seizing the territory promised them in Eastern Europe, the Soviets over the next two years remained on good terms with

Germany. Soviet raw materials sold to the Nazi regime supplied the German war machine, which overwhelmed France in 1940 and had Britain hanging by a thread in 1941. Only the German surprise attack on the Soviet Union in June 1941 ended the German-Soviet friendship. The attack drove the Soviet Union into the alliance with Great Britain and the United States, which entered the war in December 1941. But while the Soviets had been forced into the arms of the British and Americans, they found no place in the hearts of the two democracies. From the start, it was only Germany's might and murderous policies that held the Grand Alliance together.

The most important dispute between the Allies during the war was the issue of the so-called "second front." Between June 1941 and June 1944, most of the fighting in Europe was in the east between the Germans and the Soviets. The Soviet Union, which lost 20 million people during the war, suffered terrible losses in savage fighting against the Germans. Although American and British forces were fighting in Italy by 1943, defeating Germany required that the Allies land soldiers in France. From there they could threaten Germany directly and ease the terrible pressure on the Soviets. France, then, would be the crucial "second front" necessary to defeat Germany. Unfortunately, although Stalin was promised a second front in 1942, the difficulties of crossing the English Channel to invade France forced the United States and Britain to postpone the invasion twice. Each time, Stalin was furious. When the British leader, Winston Churchill, explained the first postponement to Stalin, he said, "It was like carrying a lump of ice to the North Pole."[3] The second postponement only made Stalin angrier, as Soviet losses were mounting.

3. Winston Churchill, *The Hinge of Fate, Vol. IV of The Second World War* (Boston: Houghton Mifflin, 1950), p. 475.

The second front finally became a reality on June 6, 1944, when Allied troops landed at Normandy on the French coast. By then, the postponements of the second front had become an American and British problem. The Soviets, helped enormously by shipments of U.S. weapons and other supplies, had turned the tide in the east. Their armies were pushing into several Eastern European countries formerly allied with or controlled by Germany. As the Soviets occupied those countries, they were able to control them. The same fear that had arisen in 1812 arose again: Would Russia become so powerful that it, instead of Germany, would threaten to dominate Europe? Further, if the United States and Britain became involved in an argument with the Soviets over the future of Eastern Europe, the hopes for a peaceful world once World War II was over would crumble.

To avoid these twin nightmares, the British and Americans invited the Soviets to a conference to discuss how to establish a durable peace. The meeting of the "Big Three" allies took place during February 1945, several months before Germany's final defeat, at Yalta, a resort on the Black Sea shore in the southern part of the Soviet Union. But instead of leading to a real peace, Yalta set the stage for the Cold War.

## YALTA

At Yalta, President Franklin Roosevelt represented the United States, Joseph Stalin the Soviet Union, and Winston Churchill Great Britain. Although allies, the three leaders were an odd trio. Roosevelt was a jovial, backslapping, smiling optimist who had refused to let paralysis of his legs, caused by polio, interfere with his goal of becoming president of the United States. Born to wealth and comfort, he was a hero to America's ordinary working people. When he spoke to the American people in his famous radio speeches, he addressed them as "my friends." By February 1945, however, the once vibrant Roosevelt was pale and seriously ill, with, as it would turn out, only two months more to live.

Churchill, the "British bulldog," like Roosevelt was a son of his country's wealthy upper class. In 1938 he had bitterly opposed the Munich agreement. When he came to power shortly after World War II began, he bluntly told his people he could promise them only "blood, toil, tears and sweat." Churchill's frankness, dogged strength, decisive leadership, and magnificent eloquence gave the British people courage during the darkest days of the war, as did his famous two-fingered "*V* for victory" sign.

Joseph Stalin came from a world entirely different from that of the other two leaders. He had endured grinding, brutal poverty as a youth; danger, deception, and the possibility of untimely death in the Russian revolutionary underground and in prison; and savage infighting within the Bolshevik party. Stalin was suspicious of everyone and immensely cruel. He even thought it an insult when Roosevelt casually referred to him as "Uncle Joe." His hands were stained with the blood of millions of Soviet citizens, including most of the men who had led the party to power in 1917. Both Roosevelt and Churchill knew they had to overcome Stalin's morbid and runaway suspicions if they were to lay the basis for a genuine postwar peace at Yalta. That proved to be far more difficult than the ever optimistic American leader expected or the grimly realistic British leader feared.

The meeting site at Yalta was magnificent: the summer palace of Russia's last tsar. The weather also cooperated. The sun shone brightly, and it was unusually warm for February. Prime Minister Churchill optimistically wrote,

At Yalta, Churchill, Roosevelt, and
Stalin reached agreements that helped
set the stage for postwar rivalries.

"No more let us falter! From Malta to Yalta! Let nobody alter!"[4] But falter they did, although, given the problems they faced, it is easy to understand why.

The basic problem at Yalta was that the Soviet Union came to the conference with very different goals than the United States and Britain. The most important difference concerned Poland, through which Russia had been invaded several times in its history, including in 1941. The Soviets, in order to protect themselves in the future, were determined to solidify their control over Poland. The Americans and British were just as determined to restore genuine independence to Poland, the largest country in Eastern Europe. Indeed, Britain had gone to war with Germany in 1939 when Germany invaded Poland. In 1945 neither Britain nor the United States wanted to see the Soviet Union replace Germany in Poland. That would amount to a dangerous increase in Soviet power that would threaten the nations of Western Europe and possibly lead to Soviet domination of the entire continent.

Unfortunately for the United States and Britain, at the time of the conference Soviet troops were approaching Germany's eastern borders, while the American and British advance in the west had slowed down. This left the democracies with little leverage against the Soviet Union. The situation was made even more difficult because Roosevelt needed the Soviet Union in the future. He wanted it to join in the other part of World War II, the war in the Pacific against Japan. And President Roosevelt wanted the Soviets to cooperate after the war in keeping the peace by joining a new international organization called the United Nations.

Several agreements were reached at Yalta. The Soviet Union agreed to fight Japan and join the United Nations.

4. Winston Churchill, *Triumph and Tragedy* (Boston: Houghton Mifflin, 1953), p. 338.

At the end of the war in Europe, Germany was to be divided into four occupation zones, one each for the United States, the Soviet Union, Britain, and France. The Soviet-Polish border was fixed. But the key issue was Poland's postwar government, and it was on this rock that Yalta ran aground. Although Stalin signed a vaguely worded "Declaration of Liberated Europe" that seemed to promise Poland genuinely free elections, his intent was very different. Immediately after Yalta he installed a Communist-dominated government in Poland, one totally under Soviet control. The Soviets also forced a Communist-dominated government on Romania and strengthened local Communist forces in several other Eastern European countries.

Stalin seems to have thought he could get away with this without a Western reaction. However, he was mistaken. The Western democracies reacted strongly, in part because of anger and guilt over Poland's fate and in part because they feared further Soviet advances in Eastern Europe. President Roosevelt's public statements about what he supposedly had accomplished at Yalta made things worse. Despite his concern that the Yalta agreements were too vague to guarantee Poland anything, Roosevelt had given the U.S. Congress and the American people the impression that he had saved Poland from Soviet control. So when Stalin tightened Soviet control over Poland and other Eastern European countries, American leaders and the public in general felt betrayed and grew alarmed. The Soviet Union was seen as the new aggressor in Europe. The old fears about Russian power and communism also surfaced. And when the power vacuum in Eastern Europe caused by Germany's defeat created more opportunities for Soviet expansion, the tensions and fears in the West multiplied.

Adding to the difficulties was the death of President Roosevelt, who had led the United States since 1933. Vice

President Harry Truman succeeded Roosevelt. Truman was feisty and remarkably straightforward compared with most politicians. Modest and unassuming, a man whose life-style was similar to that of many middle-class Americans of his day, Truman at first was uncomfortable being called "Mr. President." He certainly preferred "Mr. Citizen," the title he selected for his autobiography. Nor did almost eight years in the White House change this man from Missouri. In January 1953, upon signing his last official paper as president, Truman declined to take the pen he used as a souvenir, returning it instead to its place on the desk he was about to give up. The pen, the President told a surprised onlooker, "belongs to the people."

But in April 1945, when he became president, he was without experience in foreign affairs. He had not been part of Roosevelt's inner circle and therefore was poorly informed about important secret aspects of U.S. foreign policy. Yet to Harry Truman would fall the job, after the victory in World War II, of winning the peace.

# THREE

## CONTAINING SOVIET RUSSIA AND COMMUNISM

In the months after Yalta, the United States and the Soviet Union tried to work out their disagreements. Yet in less than a year, those disagreements turned into outright hostility. By 1946 the United States had abandoned its hopes of getting along with the Soviet Union in the post–World War II world. It began instead to actively oppose the expansion of Soviet power. By 1947 the new U.S. policy had a name—containment—and long-range programs to enforce it were being put into place. The Cold War had begun in earnest.

The basic cause of these developments was the power vacuum that existed in Europe after 1945 and Soviet expansion into that vacuum. As a result of World War II, the old balance of power that had given Europe some degree of stability had collapsed. Germany was defeated, divided, and occupied by the Allies. France and Britain, although on the winning side, were exhausted and badly weakened.

The rest of Europe was in a shambles. Only the Soviet Union, its terrible wartime losses notwithstanding, had any power left. Although huge parts of the western Soviet Union lay in ruins, its enormous Red Army was a mighty military machine. It occupied not only all of Poland and the eastern part of Germany, but also Romania, Bulgaria, Hungary, and part of Czechoslovakia. Soviet-controlled local Communists as yet did not completely control all of these nations, but the Red Army's presence put them under Moscow's thumb. Meanwhile, local Communist forces loyal to the Soviet Union controlled both Yugoslavia and Albania.

Making matters worse from the United States' point of view was the situation in Asia. Japan, the traditional balance to Russian power, was, like Germany, defeated and occupied. China, the region's other traditional great power, was weak, divided between bitterly opposed conservative and Communist forces, and about to plunge into civil war.

It was the opportunity to both expand the Soviet Union's influence and increase its security that Soviet dictator Joseph Stalin found irresistible. Both as Russia and the Soviet Union, his country had been invaded through Eastern Europe. Stalin was determined to prevent this from ever happening again. To this concern for security from invasion was added a fear and hatred of the capitalist West inspired by Communist ideology. Aside from Poland, the Soviets had no specific plans for the countries of Eastern Europe, other than to prevent hostile governments from gaining power and to maximize Communist influence there. But Stalin soon began to tighten his grip on a region that the harsh fortunes of war had brought into his grasp. He did so in part because the West did little more than send angry notes with each Soviet advance. Later, as tensions grew greater, the Soviets clamped down even harder to avoid losing the valuable prize World War II had given them at such a high price.

In short, whatever their fears of each other, in the days immediately after World War II both the West and the Soviet Union were basically on the defensive. Neither the Western Allies nor the Soviet Union wanted to ruin the chances for a stable postwar peace. But each side wanted peace on its own terms. And the Soviet terms—control of Eastern Europe—were seen by the Western democracies as a promise of further Soviet expansion and therefore a direct threat to their security. This combination of ingredients was a formula for conflict, not genuine peace.

## POTSDAM AND THE ATOMIC BOMB

In July 1945 the Big Three leaders met again at Potsdam, a suburb of bombed-out Berlin. Despite several agreements reached after difficult negotiations, the conference left the new American president, Harry Truman, convinced that Stalin was an "SOB" and that the Soviet Union would listen only to force. Potsdam is also notable because at the time of the conference the world changed forever when the United States successfully tested an awesome new weapon, the atomic bomb. The atomic bomb brought about Japan's surrender, after it was dropped on Hiroshima on August 6 and Nagasaki on August 9. However, it did nothing to make the Soviets loosen their hold on Eastern Europe, as some Western observers hoped it might.

The decision to drop the atomic bomb on Japan was the most controversial one of World War II. Harry Truman, the man who made it, had been president only a few months when he unleashed a weapon that killed 80,000 people in a single blast at Hiroshima. Some historians have accused Truman of using the atomic bomb as an opening salvo in the Cold War, to impress the Soviets and force them to compromise on their control over Poland. This accusation is unfair and false. The decision to use the atomic bomb was the last decision of World War II, not the first of the Cold War. The United States had suffered enormous casualties in driving the Japanese from territory they had overrun, and Japanese resistance was becoming fiercer as they were driven closer to their home islands. Truman ordered the bomb to be used to shorten the war and avoid even higher American casualties. As he explained it, in his usual direct style, "Let there be no mistake about it. I regarded the bomb as a military weapon and never had any doubt that it should be used."[1]

Of course, both the President and his top advisers hoped that the atomic bomb would help the United States in the postwar era. Truman knew that as soon as the war was over, pressure at home would force him to demobilize most of the U.S. Army. This would leave the Red Army as the major military force on the European continent, with only the U.S. arsenal of a few atomic bombs to balance it. Still, President Truman's concern in August 1945 was to use the bomb to defeat Japan, not threaten the Soviet Union.

## THE IRON CURTAIN SPEECH

Japan surrendered in September 1945, officially ending World War II. Without a common enemy to unite them, the Soviet Union and the United States quickly drew apart. By January, President Truman had written to his secretary of state: "Unless Russia is faced with an iron fist and strong language another war is in the making. Only one language

1. Quoted in Stephen Ambrose, *Rise to Globalism: American Foreign Policy, 1938–1976* (New York: Penguin, 1976), p. 99.

do they understand—'how many divisions have you?' ...
I'm tired of babying the Russians."[2] Meanwhile, in February 1946, Stalin delivered a widely publicized, hard-line speech. The response from the West came on March 5, 1946, in Fulton, Missouri. At Truman's invitation and with the President sitting on the platform behind him, Churchill gave the speech that in effect announced the coming of the Cold War. Churchill, eloquent and brilliant whether speaking or writing, drew a grim picture of the postwar situation caused by Soviet expansion in Eastern Europe:

> *A shadow has fallen upon the scenes so lately lighted by the Allied victory. . . . From Stettin in the Baltic to Trieste in the Adriatic, an iron curtain has descended across the Continent. Behind that line lie all the capitals of the ancient states of Central and Eastern Europe. Warsaw, Berlin, Prague, Vienna, Budapest, Belgrade, Bucharest, and Sophia, all these famous cities . . . lie in what I must call the Soviet sphere, and all are subject in one form or another . . . to a very high and, in many cases, increasing measure of control from Moscow. . . . This is certainly not the liberated Europe we sought to build up. Nor is it one which contains the essentials of a permanent peace.*[3]

Truman agreed with Churchill. The President was deeply worried, and his anxiety increased as the year wore on. Soviet pressure on two non-European countries—Iran and Turkey—led to direct U.S.-Soviet confrontations. In both cases the Soviets backed down. In the Iranian crisis a

2. Quoted in John Lewis Gaddis, *The United States and the Origins of the Cold War* (New York: Columbia University Press, 1972), p. 289.

3. Quoted in Louis Halle, *The Cold War as History* (New York: Harper & Row, 1962), pp. 103–4.

strongly worded note from the United States did the job, but the Turkish incident was not resolved until Truman sent a powerful U.S. aircraft carrier into the eastern Mediterranean to back the Turks. Two American proposals for United Nations control of atomic weapons died of fatal doses of mutual Soviet-American mistrust. There were continual crises in Germany, where Soviet occupiers clashed with American, British, and French occupiers. Although the Soviets still permitted some non-Communist political parties to exist in Eastern Europe, their military grip on the region remained firm.

Communist political parties were doing well outside the Soviet zone of control. In France and Italy they were powerful enough to participate in the governments of those countries as part of a coalition of political parties. In Greece, Communist guerrillas were waging a vicious civil war against the British-backed conservative government. In distant China, the country with the largest population in the world, another Communist-inspired civil war raged.

## THE TRUMAN DOCTRINE, THE MARSHALL PLAN, AND CONTAINMENT

The most urgent crisis was in Greece. Only British intervention in the late days of World War II had prevented a Communist takeover of that country. However, the British-installed government was corrupt and undemocratic. By the fall of 1946, Communist guerrillas again were fighting for control of Greece. In February 1947 the British told the United States that they could no longer afford to back the tottering Greek government. Britain, the only country that had fought the Germans from the first day of both World War I and World War II to the last, was too exhausted to fight, or to pay, anymore.

In the bitter Greek civil war, Communist
guerrillas fought government forces—but it was
often hard to tell friend from foe. This battalion
is made up of former guerrillas who switched
sides to fight for the government.

President Truman was convinced the United States had to act. He feared that a Communist victory in Greece would bring Soviet power into the Mediterranean Sea, astride shipping routes to the oil-rich Middle East. It would outflank the West's line of defense in Europe and put enormous pressure on Italy, which lies across the Adriatic Sea from Greece. There was a real danger that the Italian Communist party, the largest in the West, might come to power through elections. France, which also had a powerful Communist party, might then be destabilized, while to the east the fall of Greece would be felt in both Turkey and Iran.

While all this was happening, Truman had few means to combat Communist advances in Europe and Asia. During 1946 and into 1947 the United States conducted the largest and fastest demobilization in history. Its Army shrank from over eight million to barely one million men. Of the few remaining U.S. troops in Europe, most were inexperienced new draftees. The Navy and Air Force had been similarly cut. The U.S. defense budget had been cut even more deeply, leaving the President without financial resources to help the Greek government. At home the American people, after four years of war, had little interest in foreign affairs and the growing emergency in Europe.

On March 12, 1947, the President spoke to a joint session of Congress. He discussed not only the Communist threat to Greece but what he said was a serious situation in Turkey. Truman pictured a world divided into free and totalitarian countries and stressed that the United States would not be secure in a world dominated by the latter. That was why, the President insisted, the United States had to help Greece and Turkey:

*We shall not realize our objectives ... unless we are willing to help free peoples to maintain their free institutions and national integrity against ag-*

*gressive movements that seek to impose upon them totalitarian regimes. This is no more than a frank recognition that totalitarian regimes imposed upon free peoples by direct or indirect aggression undermine the foundations of international peace and hence the security of the United States.*[4]

Truman specifically asked for $300 million for Greece and $100 million for Turkey, which Congress provided. The President's speech, however, amounted to much more than that. It took American foreign policy in a clearly internationalist direction and changed that policy as it had existed from the time of George Washington. For the first time the United States was intervening in the affairs of a country outside the Western Hemisphere during peacetime. Beyond that, Truman's speech and Congress's support of it implied an American commitment to help countries worldwide resist Communist aggression or subversion. That commitment was called the Truman Doctrine.

American aid soon helped turn the tide in Greece, and the Communist rebellion was defeated. But Truman and his advisers became convinced that the aid package to Greece and Turkey was not nearly enough to stop Communist expansion in Europe. Although the war in Europe had been over for two years, the expected recovery in Western Europe had not taken place. American aid and a variety of loans had not helped nearly enough. Instead, it seemed as if several large Western European societies were on the verge of collapse and that another fertile field for Communist advance was opening up. In Britain the harsh winter of 1946–1947 had crippled the economy. Half

4. Quoted in James A. Nathan and James K. Oliver, *United States Foreign Policy and World Order*, 4th ed. (Glenview, Ill.: Scott, Foresman, 1989), p. 56.

of the factories were closed. Coal mines had closed down, leaving the country without essential fuel for running factories and heating homes. In France the bitterly cold winter cut short a recovery and destroyed crops, leaving the cities short of food. The worst conditions, however, were in Germany, the economic giant of non-Communist Europe before the Nazis had unleashed World War II and its horrors upon the world. One historian described the situation this way:

> *The measure of Germany's collapse was indicated by the fact that the cigarette had replaced money as the prevailing unit of exchange. Cigarettes could buy almost anything. . . . A package of cigarettes was equivalent to a working man's entire wages for a month. . . . Everywhere people were hungry. . . . Respectable girls sold their bodies for one or two cigarettes, a pair of nylons, or an army ration; dishonor was preferable to death. Juvenile delinquency increased and stealing became a respectable way of earning a living for boys as did prostitution for girls.[5]*

The advance of communism was only one danger. If Western European nations could not feed themselves, they could hardly buy American-made goods. Because Western Europe was America's largest export market, this would hurt American industries and cause unemployment and economic hardship in the United States. The U.S. government therefore began to devise a new program, called the Marshall Plan after Secretary of State George C. Marshall, a general and hero of World War II, who announced it in July 1947. Marshall called for the United States to give— not lend—the nations of Europe $20 *billion* to revive their

5. John A. Spanier, *American Foreign Policy Since World War II*, 10th ed. (New York: Holt, Rinehart and Winston, 1985), p. 35.

economies. The amount of money he suggested was an enormous sum, almost twice the U.S. defense budget and equal to hundreds of billions of dollars today. Marshall also called on the European nations, including America's former enemy Germany, to work together to rebuild their economies. Not surprisingly, Congress was shocked by what Marshall was asking for, and at first refused to provide the money.

It took a deepening of the Cold War to get Congress to act. Marshall had invited *all* European countries to participate in the U.S. plan, including the nations of Eastern Europe and the Soviet Union. The Soviets opposed this because close economic ties with Western Europe could gradually pry Eastern Europe out of the Soviet grasp. Their concern focused on Czechoslovakia, and their actions soon created yet another crisis in Europe.

By 1947, Soviet control over Eastern Europe was total, except in Czechoslovakia. Before it was abandoned to Germany at the Munich conference in 1938, Czechoslovakia had been the only democracy in Eastern Europe. After the war, democracy was reestablished in Czechoslovakia. Although its government was not a Soviet-controlled Communist dictatorship as in the rest of Eastern Europe, Czechoslovakia seemed to meet the conditions the Soviets insisted they needed for their security. It was friendly to the Soviet Union, and it had a powerful Communist party that participated in the government. However, Czechoslovakia wanted to participate in the Marshall Plan. This slight deviation from Soviet dictates was unacceptable to Stalin, who feared any Western influence anywhere in Eastern Europe. Therefore, on February 25, 1948, the Soviets sponsored a coup in Czechoslovakia that overthrew the democratic government and established a Communist dictatorship under Soviet control.

The Communist coup in Czechoslovakia shocked Western Europe and the United States. Everybody remembered 1938; it seemed too much to bear that only ten

Through the Marshall Plan, American aid helps
restore a building on the Kurfurstendamm,
one of Berlin's main avenues.

years later democratic Czechoslovakia once again was being destroyed by a totalitarian aggressor. This new and brutal Soviet advance frightened and angered even the skeptics in the Congress who had opposed the Marshall Plan. In March, Congress funded the first installment of the Plan, and the rebuilding of Western Europe began. By the time it ended in 1952, the Marshall Plan provided more than $12 billion to rebuild Western Europe. It succeeded beyond even the most optimistic predictions and undoubtedly was the single most successful U.S. foreign policy program of the Cold War.

The Truman Doctrine and Marshall Plan were the first steps in the new U.S. Cold War foreign policy known as containment. The term *containment* was first used publicly in 1947 in an article by George Kennan, a State Department expert on the Soviet Union. The policy assumed that the Soviet Union was by its very nature driven to expand. Communist ideology was totally hostile to Western capitalism and democracy and determined to destroy it. In addition, using techniques drawn from prerevolutionary Russian history, the Soviets would patiently await opportunities and expand until they met resistance. They would then pause, but only pause, and await new opportunities to expand. Kennan outlined how to meet that constant threat:

> *In these circumstances it is clear that the main element of any United States policy toward the Soviet Union must be that of a long-term, patient but firm and vigilant containment of Russian expansive tendencies.*[6]

The Truman Doctrine, which included both economic and military aid, and the Marshall Plan, a program of economic

6. George Kennan, "The Sources of Soviet Conduct," *Foreign Affairs*, July 1947, p. 575.

aid, were the first containment policies. During the Cold War the United States used many means—military, economic, political—to carry out containment. Although the tactics sometimes changed, containment remained the U.S. strategy for dealing with the Soviet Union until the end of the Cold War.

## THE BERLIN BLOCKADE

Before the Marshall Plan could have an impact, Stalin made a drastic and very dangerous attempt to discredit the United States in the eyes of the Europeans who were turning to Washington for help. By 1948, Joseph Stalin in Moscow was just as unhappy about the situation in Europe as was Harry Truman in Washington. Stalin wanted to keep Germany weak and out of the Western camp, but the United States, Britain, and France were taking steps to combine their three zones into a unified and anti-Communist West Germany. Stalin wanted to see Western Europe remain in crisis, as a weak Western Europe strengthened the Soviet position on the continent. But the United States was taking steps toward rebuilding Western Europe.

Stalin also wanted absolute control of Eastern Europe, but even that was slipping beyond his grasp. By 1948, he was quarreling with Josip Broz Tito, the Communist dictator of Yugoslavia. Because he had come to power without Soviet help, Tito was not Stalin's puppet. The result of the quarrel was that Yugoslavia broke away from the Soviet bloc and became neutral in the Soviet-American Cold War struggle. Aside from his fury over failing to control Yugoslavia, Stalin was worried about how the Yugoslav example would affect the rest of his European empire.

Stalin blamed the United States for all his troubles. He therefore decided the time had come to do two things: stop the formation of a West German state and undermine American influence in all of Europe. His strategy was simple: show the people of Europe that they could not count on the United States in a real crisis. In particular, prove that the United States would not stand up to the Soviet Union when the chips were down. If that could be done, perhaps first the Germans and then America's allies in Western Europe would try to cut the best deal they could with the Soviet Union, rather than relying on the United States. After all, the Soviet Union was in the middle of Europe with the largest army on the continent, while the United States was 3,000 miles (4,800 kilometers) away.

Stalin made his move in Berlin, which was surrounded by the Soviet occupation zone. On June 24, 1948, the Soviet Union announced a complete blockade of all land routes leading to Berlin. Since the three Western zones of Berlin were totally isolated from all supplies, Stalin expected that the United States and its British and French allies would be forced to leave Berlin. There seemed to be no way to supply the city. If the United States tried to shoot its way into Berlin, it might well start World War III. Using force therefore was out. None of this fazed President Truman. He bluntly told his advisers, "We're going to stay, period."

With all ground routes blocked, the only way to supply Berlin was by air. This seemed impossible. How could a city of 2.5 million people—the fifth-largest city in the world at the time—be supplied by aircraft alone with enough food, fuel, clothing, and other essentials people used in their daily lives? Yet it was done. An assortment of airplanes carried everything from coal to eggs to hungry West Berlin. Eventually over seven thousand tons of supplies reached Berlin daily, arriving on planes that landed every ninety seconds during peak hours:

*The droning of motors overhead never stopped.*
*Berliners . . . would never forget the endlessness of*

*it. Bright days and cloudy, in fog and in pitch-black night, the noise was there. . . . The burdened planes lurched off or slammed down on runways in a permanent parade of overwork. . . . The pilots set them down in Berlin, and men and trucks swarmed around the aircraft and quickly emptied their bellies of sacks of coal, cartons of dried milk and potatoes and eggs, medicine, blankets, and essential spare parts for the machinery that kept a modern city going. Then they took off immediately for the bases at Frankfurt and Hamburg to descend into another maelstrom of mechanics, who were squirting oil, pouring gas, changing sparkplugs, gaskets, and fittings, at a mad tempo, while loading crews jostled their elbows. And then the sturdy planes were airborne again.[7]*

Inside the surrounded city, the people survived on daily rations of 17 ounces (482 grams) of bread and even smaller portions of a few other foods. The Soviet Union was stymied. It could easily have shot down the Allied planes, but that would have started the dreaded war that neither side wanted. In June 1949, Stalin gave in. The Berlin Airlift had defeated the Berlin Blockade.

## 1949: NATO, THE BOMB, AND THE FALL OF CHINA

The first part of 1949 went well for the United States. In April, just before the Western triumph in Berlin, the United States, Britain, France, and eight other nations signed a treaty creating a military alliance called the North

7. Bernard A. Weisberger, *Cold War, Cold Peace: The United States and Russia Since 1945* (New York: American Heritage, 1984), p. 92.

**West Berlin children watch an American plane
arrive during the Berlin Airlift.**

Atlantic Treaty Organization (NATO). NATO was an unmistakable sign that the United States intended to back its allies in Europe. It also marked yet another historic change in U.S. foreign policy. By joining NATO, the United States entered a peacetime military alliance for the first time in its history. Meanwhile, in May, the three Western zones of Germany were combined into the new Federal Republic of Germany (West Germany), with its capital in Bonn on the Rhine River. The next month brought the West's victory in Berlin.

However, the second half of the year brought grim news. In August the Soviet Union exploded its first atomic bomb. The American monopoly of nuclear weapons, which was seen as the balance against the Red Army, was over after only four years. In October, Communist forces emerged victorious after a three-year civil war in China, despite $2 billion in U.S. aid to anti-Communist forces. In one blow, one-fourth of the world's population fell under Communist rule. Just as containment seemed to be succeeding in Europe, the Communist tide surged forward in a gigantic wave in Asia. Cold War victories were being matched by Cold War defeats. And a new crisis, this one in the small northeast Asian country of Korea, was about to add a hot war to what already was a boiling pot.

# FOUR

## THE KOREAN WAR

Korea, an ancient country, occupies a peninsula in northeast Asia that extends about 400 miles (640 kilometers) from China into the Gulf of Japan. Often in its 2,000-year history Korea has been caught in struggles between China and Japan, its larger and more powerful neighbors. Korea has struggled to maintain its independence from China and has fought off Japanese raids and invasions. It has become a battleground between the Chinese and Japanese on several occasions. In the 1590s the Chinese defeated the Japanese in Korea, while in the 1890s the Japanese emerged victorious.

By the late nineteenth century another power, Russia, was becoming interested in Korea. Tension between the expanding Russian and Japanese empires in northeast Asia eventually led to the Russo-Japanese war of 1904–1905. After their victory the triumphant Japanese tightened their grip on Korea. A Korean rebellion against Japanese imperialism was unsuccessful, and in 1910 Japan formally turned Korea into a Japanese colony. The Japanese treated the Koreans with extreme brutality until Japan's defeat in World War II finally ousted it from the peninsula.

The end of World War II brought no relief to Korea. In 1945, largely for reasons of convenience in arranging the surrender of Japanese troops on the peninsula, the country was divided in half. North of the 38th parallel the Soviet Union disarmed the Japanese, while south of that line the United States did the job. Plans called for Korea to be reunited after nationwide elections. However, the early frosts of the Cold War killed Korean unification.

Instead of allowing the elections, which would have ended Soviet control on the Korean peninsula, in 1947 the Soviets installed a Communist government under the dictator Kim Il-Sung. The United States then held elections in its occupation zone, which were won by a pro-American politician named Syngman Rhee. Rhee was a well-known Korean nationalist with a fairly strong political base. He also had little tolerance for those who disagreed with him. Although he was not a totalitarian dictator like Kim, his regime could hardly be called democratic. After he became Korea's president, Rhee arrested thousands of his opponents and became increasingly unpopular.

As the 1950s dawned, two hostile Korean states— Communist North Korea and anti-Communist South Korea—faced each other on their narrow peninsula. In the north, Kim waited impatiently with a well-equipped, Soviet-trained army for his chance to reunify Korea under his control. Although Rhee's army was poorly equipped, he also was determined to reunify Korea, but as an anti-Communist state. The Korean peninsula was a tinderbox, just waiting for a spark to explode into flames.

Several events in the first half of 1950 increased the tension. In January, U.S. secretary of state Dean Acheson made a speech in which he failed to list Korea among the regions the United States would defend in northeast Asia. A few months later a leading U.S. senator went further when he suggested that Korea could not be defended militarily and might have to be abandoned. Meanwhile, South Korean president Rhee's party suffered a major election defeat, despite strong-arm tactics that included arrests of over twenty of his leading political opponents.

Kim Il-Sung decided the time to strike had come. Stalin and the Soviet Union had given him the arms he needed. Although Stalin seems not to have known Kim was poised to attack South Korea, the Soviet leader had done nothing to discourage his Korean ally and everything to make his aggression possible. So at 4 o'clock on the morning of June 25, 1950, 75,000 heavily armed North Korean troops swept across the 38th parallel. It quickly became clear that the lightly armed South Koreans could do nothing to stop them, despite President Rhee's boasting to the contrary in the months just before the invasion.

The news of the North Korean invasion shocked and worried President Truman. The fall of China in 1949 had left Japan face-to-face with the world's two Communist giants, the Soviet Union and the People's Republic of China (PRC). A Communist advance in Korea, which the Japanese considered a "dagger" pointed at their country, would greatly strengthen Communist forces among the Japanese and undermine the American effort to build a democratic Japan allied to the West. In addition, Truman and his advisers viewed the invasion as sponsored by the Soviet Union to test the United States' willingness to defend its interests in Asia. The President was convinced that American prestige was at stake. The United States could not let Communist forces simply invade and take over a small, weak country. If it did, that would encourage further Communist aggression and only make matters worse. As

Truman put it, "This [Korea] is the Greece of the Far East. If we are tough enough now, there won't be any next step."[1]

The President's strategy was to take the Korean crisis to the UN Security Council. His timing was excellent. The Soviet Union was not present because it was boycotting the United Nations for refusing to recognize the PRC as the legitimate government of China. The Soviets therefore were unable to veto a U.S.-sponsored resolution that labeled North Korea as an aggressor. The United States immediately began sending supplies to help the South Koreans. It also used warplanes to try to stop the invaders. But neither supplies nor bombs could stop them. Armed with a second UN resolution calling on members to defend South Korea, Truman reached what he later called the most difficult decision of his presidency. Gambling that neither the Soviet Union nor China would send its own troops into Korea, he decided to send U.S. soldiers to fight there.

The President did not, however, go to Congress for a declaration of war. Instead, the Korean War officially became a UN "police action" in which aggression was to be resisted by the United Nations as a whole. In reality, almost all the air and naval forces on the UN side came from the United States, as well as most of the money to fight the war. While a number of American allies sent some troops into combat—among them Great Britain, France, Turkey, Greece, and the Philippines—half of the UN troops were Americans, and most of the rest were South Koreans. Official language notwithstanding, the conflict in Korea was very much a war, and a bitter, costly, and frustrating war at that.

1. Quoted in Beverly Smith, "The White House Story: Why We Went to War in Korea," *Saturday Evening Post*, November 10, 1951, p. 80.

Truman sent General Douglas MacArthur, a World War II hero, to Korea to stop the Communists. After nearly being pushed off the Korean peninsula entirely, in September MacArthur counterattacked behind the North Korean lines. Cut off from their supply lines, the North Koreans fled northward in panic, across the 38th parallel. At that point Truman decided to let MacArthur cross the old border in pursuit and drive northward to the Yalu River, Korea's border with the People's Republic of China, thereby liberating all of Korea from communism. The decision was a gamble, because China had warned it would intervene if UN troops approached the Yalu. In addition, in 1950 the Soviet Union had signed a mutual defense treaty with China, so it was possible that it too might be drawn into the Korean conflict. That raised the prospect that the Korean War could lead to World War III.

The worst-case scenario—Soviet involvement—did not occur, but what did happen was bad enough. In November 300,000 Chinese troops were thrown into the battle. Once again the UN troops were pushed south of the 38th parallel. Truman now went back to his original objective, to reach the 38th parallel and restore a non-Communist South Korea. The Korean War turned from an apparent quick victory into a grinding hill-by-hill struggle that lasted until 1953. Bloody Ridge and Heartbreak Hill, two names U.S. soldiers gave to barren hills 3 miles (5 kilometers) apart, grimly tell what kind of war it was.

Making matters worse, MacArthur disagreed with Truman's decision to merely return to the 38th parallel. The flamboyant general wanted to liberate all of Korea and bomb China to help drive its troops from the peninsula. MacArthur felt so strongly about this that he violated military discipline and publicly criticized President Truman. The general rejected the President's policy with the famous line "There is no substitute for victory." This open

**Troops of the U.S. 1st Cavalry Division march
north toward the 38th parallel in 1951.**

defiance left President Truman no choice. He had to affirm what the U.S. Constitution makes clear: that under the U.S. system of government the civilian president controls the military. In April 1951 Truman fired MacArthur, causing an uproar among the general's supporters in the United States.

The fighting in Korea then dragged on for over two more years. The long struggle without a clear victory weakened Truman and his Democratic party at home and contributed to a Republican victory in the 1952 presidential election. The new president who took office in 1953 was General Dwight D. Eisenhower, the commander of all Allied forces in Europe during World War II. The Eisenhower administration was determined to end the war and secretly hinted that it might use atomic weapons against Communist forces if a cease-fire was not reached.

The Soviet Union, which had backed the North Koreans and Chinese, also wanted an end to the fighting. Joseph Stalin had died in March of 1953, and his successors wanted to reduce tensions with the United States so they could focus on their many problems at home. The Korean cease-fire agreement was signed on July 27, 1953, in a wooden hut at Panmunjom, a barren village near the 38th parallel. The bitterness in the hut could be cut with a knife. After the signing, not a word was said. Representatives of the two sides simply turned away from each other and left.

The Korean War took more than 54,000 American lives. No less than two million Koreans, and perhaps twice that number, also died, as well as hundreds of thousands of Chinese. Korea, both north and south, was left in ruins. General MacArthur described what he saw in 1951, two years before the fighting ended:

*The war in Korea ... almost destroyed that nation. ... I have seen, I guess, as much blood and*

In the Korean countryside, the war developed into a
bloody hill-by-hill struggle. Here, U.S. soldiers have taken
a ridge and fire on North Korean positions below.

*disaster as any living man, and it just curdled my*
*stomach, the last time I was there. After I looked at*
*that wreckage and those thousands of women and*
*children and everything, I vomited.*[2]

The border between North and South Korea remained largely unchanged near the 38th parallel, with South Korea having gained a small amount of territory. And although the 1953 cease-fire ended the fighting in Korea, no formal peace treaty ever officially ended the war.

In terms of the larger Cold War, the military stalemate in Korea meant that for the United States containment of Communism in Europe had been matched by containment in Asia. However, during the Korean conflict the Cold War intensified. United States defense spending quadrupled between 1950 and 1953 to about $60 billion per year. The money paid not only for UN soldiers in Korea, but for an overall program of U.S. rearmament. That program included sending thousands of troops to Western Europe, where they joined other NATO troops standing guard against the Soviet Union.

In addition, the Korean War poisoned relations between the United States and the newly established People's Republic of China. When Communist forces led by Mao Zedong drove the old Nationalist government from the Chinese mainland in 1949, the future of Chinese-U.S. relations was unclear. Mao Zedong did not get along with Stalin, and the Soviets had provided the Chinese Communist party with very little help in its struggle for power. Some American policymakers hoped to establish diplomatic relations with the PRC, and to encourage it to take a neutral stance in the Soviet-American Cold War. After all,

2. U.S. Congress, Senate Committee on Armed Services and Committee on Foreign Relations, *Hearings on the Military Situation in the Far East*, 82nd Congress, 1st Session, 1951, pp. 3075, 3082.

although both the Chinese and the Soviets called themselves Communists, Russia and China had a long history of rivalry.

That hope was shattered as soon as the Korean War began. One of President Truman's first actions was to send the U.S. Navy to protect what was left of the Nationalist government. It had taken refuge on the island of Formosa (now known as Taiwan), 110 miles (175 kilometers) from the Chinese mainland. Despite the tiny territory they controlled, the Nationalists claimed to be the legitimate government of all of China. The United States, with its navy in the strait between Formosa and the mainland, supported that claim and refused to recognize the PRC. As a result, normal relations between the United States and PRC were not established until 1979.

Still, the Korean War finally was over. Both the United States and the Soviet Union had new leaders. Both sides hoped to improve the icy relations between them. That hope would flicker briefly, and then succumb to the chilling winds of the deepening Cold War.

# FIVE

## THE COLD WAR UNDERGROUND
## AND AT HOME

While well-publicized Cold War crises were making daily headlines, secret schemes that were equally part of the struggle were unfolding out of sight. They were acted out in the shadowy and often deadly world of spies and counterspies, coups and assassinations, and acts of sabotage and murder. Periodically these underground burrowings broke through to the surface. When that happened, especially if they involved spying by the Soviet Union during the early days of the Cold War, many Americans became afraid. The idea of facing an enemy like Soviet communism out in the open was bad enough. But the thought that Soviet secret agents were prowling around the United States was enough to inflame existing fears until they burned out of control. These fears were based on a vastly exaggerated view of Soviet activities in the United States. Nonetheless, they contributed to a so-called "red scare" that began in the late 1940s and peaked during what is known as the McCarthy era of the early 1950s.

Fear of nuclear war was widespread in the 1950s. In civil-defense drills (left), children were instructed to "duck and cover" in the event of an attack. To survive a nuclear attack, families were encouraged to install prefabricated underground bomb shelters (above).

The red scare actually was a reaction to much more than Soviet spying. In the years after 1945, many Americans were frustrated when the United States, the most powerful country in the world, had so much trouble getting its way in international conflicts. First Eastern Europe had fallen to communism, then China. The Soviet Union successfully tested its first atomic bomb well ahead of most predictions. And the United States, whose forces had defeated the mighty military machines of Germany and Japan, was unable to win a decisive victory in Korea. How, frightened Americans asked, could this all happen?

Many people, egged on by politicians willing to exploit their fears, grasped at a simple explanation: Communists somehow had infiltrated the U.S. government and were manipulating its foreign policy, causing one U.S. defeat after another. This was nonsense, but all too often the facts did not matter. Within two years after the defeat of Nazism, a frantic hunt for alleged Communists in positions of influence had begun. Self-appointed Communist hunters in Washington and across the country damaged the reputations of thousands of Americans, whose basic constitutional rights were violated by wild accusations and unfair investigations. People were fired from their jobs or prevented from getting work simply because they held or were suspected of holding unpopular or controversial views. Public figures who disagreed with these witch hunts, including President Truman, often failed to oppose them strongly enough, lest they give the impression they were "soft" on communism and lose the next election.

## SPIES AND COUNTERSPIES

Although many Americans associated spying, sabotage, and similar activities solely with the Soviet Union, the fact was that the United States participated in them as well. For example, in 1947 it set up the Central Intelligence Agency (CIA) to gather information and carry out other secret operations in foreign nations. Between 1949 and 1954 the CIA infiltrated agents by land, sea, and even parachute into the Soviet Union in a program named operation Red Sox/Red Cap. The agents were ex–Soviet citizens who were expected to blend in with the general population. However, the operation suffered high losses and produced limited results.

The CIA's operation in Berlin was far more successful. While the Berlin Wall built by the Soviets in 1961 is famous, few people know about the Berlin tunnel built by the CIA in 1955. It ran for 500 yards (460 meters) from the edge of West Berlin to underground telephone cables leading from Soviet military headquarters in East Berlin. Until the Soviets discovered it in 1956, American agents in the comfortable, air-conditioned, and soundproofed tunnel were able to tap into top-secret Soviet communications.

Another successful American spy program took place in the air, although at a high price. During the 1950s and 1960s the United States sent more than ten thousand air spy missions against the Soviet Union. Many missions were flown inside Soviet airspace, often in unarmed aircraft, and some were shot down. When that happened, because the U.S. government did not want to admit to the flights, sometimes nothing was done to recover possible survivors. Of over 250 U.S. fliers shot down between 1950 and 1970, 24 died and 138 have never been accounted for. As one aide to President Eisenhower put it, "Our planes didn't have speed, and often were unarmed and the Soviets would pick us off. So we lost a lot of our boys."[1] One U.S. plane that flew quickly was a specially designed aircraft called the U-2. Between 1956 and 1960, American U-2 spy planes traveled deep inside the Soviet Union. Armed with high-

1. Quoted in *U.S. News and World Report*, March 15, 1993, p. 34.

powered cameras and flying so high that Soviet antiaircraft weapons could not reach them, the U-2s brought back invaluable information about Soviet military strength. However, in 1960 newly developed Soviet missiles shot down a U-2, and the resulting publicity destroyed an upcoming summit meeting between President Eisenhower and Soviet premier Nikita Khrushchev.

American efforts were more than matched by a Soviet spy network that was by far the largest in the world. Because the United States was an open society, it was relatively easy for the Soviets to place and recruit spies inside their capitalist rival. The Soviet spy network was run primarily by two agencies, the secret police (or Committee for State Security, known by its Russian acronym, KGB, since the 1950s) and Soviet military intelligence (the Chief Directorate of Intelligence, or GRU). Soviet spy efforts were often assisted by the willing participation of citizens of Western countries, including the United States. Some of these people believed that communism was the true hope for mankind and that by helping the Soviet Union, even if they were betraying their own countries, they were serving all of humanity.

The Soviets had some stunning successes during the early days of the Cold War. Perhaps the most important was the theft of top-secret information about how to build an atomic bomb. Klaus Fuchs, a German-born scientist who worked on secret nuclear research projects in both Great Britain and the United States, provided information during the late 1940s that speeded up Soviet work on the bomb by at least two years. In fact, the first atomic bomb tested by the Soviet Union was based on information Fuchs provided. A few years later, the Soviets successfully tested a bomb of their own design.

Another spectacular Soviet success was to place agents deep within the British intelligence network. British-born and from privileged backgrounds, these

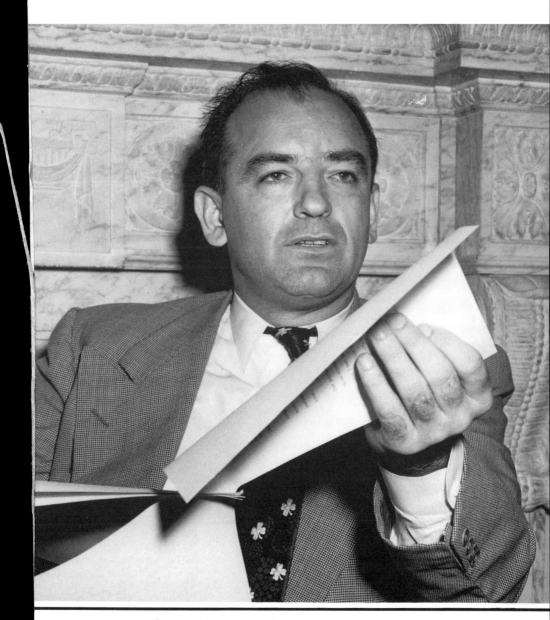

Senator Joseph McCarthy conducted what
amounted to a witch-hunt against people
he accused of being Communists.

*Some men of little minds and less morals are today using the Korean War as a profitable political diversion, a vehicle by which to build up battered reputations because of incompetence and worse.[3]*

With language like that, McCarthy stained not only the United States Senate but also American political life in the 1950s. When several senators who opposed McCarthy were defeated in the 1952 elections, McCarthy's influence and ability to damage innocent people grew. Not until he attacked the U.S. Army for being soft on communism did McCarthy finally reach too far. Millions of Americans watched McCarthy investigate the Army firsthand by means of a device that was just entering American living rooms—television. What filled their tiny black-and-white screens was a cruel and uncontrollable bully willing to use any sordid tactic to smear his opponents. McCarthy's reputation plummeted. The Senate found the courage to censure him for improper conduct. Three years later McCarthy was dead from liver disease caused by excessive alcohol consumption.

After McCarthy was discredited, the anti-Communist hysteria slowly subsided. But many innocent Americans already had seen their careers and lives damaged simply because they held unpopular views or were suspected of doing so. Many more found it wise to keep their views to themselves rather than risk being labeled a Communist or pro-Communist. The United States was fighting the Cold War to preserve its freedoms. But the fears the Cold War helped cause at home during the 1940s and 1950s undermined some of those freedoms, even as the Soviet enemy abroad was successfully being contained and held at bay.

3. U.S. Congress, *Senate Congressional Record*, 81st Congress, 2nd session, 1950, 96, pp. 9715–9716.

## NEW LEADERS AND
## NEW PROBLEMS

The year 1953 marked the start of a new phase in the Cold War, one that began with an unexpectedly clean slate. Along with the end of the Korean War, 1953 brought both the United States and the Soviet Union new leaders. Of the two superpowers, the United States politically was in a far more secure position. Its new president, Dwight David Eisenhower, was an enormously popular war hero with considerable experience in foreign affairs. He had been elected in an orderly fashion according to the law of the land, and both his powers and his term of office were clear. The Soviet Union, on the other hand, was not even entirely sure who its new leader was, how long he might remain in office, and how powerful he would be. Stalin, the tyrannical and murderous dictator for a generation, had not designated a successor. Several men, while publicly committed to working together, were privately vying for the top spot.

At first, Georgi Malenkov, Stalin's right-hand man during the dictator's last years, emerged as the apparent new number one. However, his star began to fade before 1953 was over, and by 1955 a tough, feisty, barrel-shaped, peasant-born former mine worker named Nikita Khrushchev had pushed Malenkov aside. A second round in the struggle for power confirmed Khrushchev's victory in 1957.

With Stalin finally gone, the Soviet Union began to change. The one thing that every contender for power agreed on was that there should never be another Stalin. With his absolute power, Stalin had terrorized the entire country, including the men around him. Whoever ended up as number one would not be permitted to have the power Stalin had. There also had to be other reforms, most importantly a rise in the Soviet Union's miserably low standard of living. Because there was so much to do inside the Soviet Union, Stalin's successors wanted to reduce tensions with the United States.

## EISENHOWER'S "NEW LOOK"

Despite new leadership, both the United States and the Soviet Union still held the basic attitudes toward each other that had produced the Cold War. The United States continued its policy of containment against communism in general and the Soviet Union in particular. However, Eisenhower believed that the United States was spending too much money on its military in order to carry out containment. If this continued, the President worried, it would undermine the welfare of the nation. As he remarked just before he left office: "Every gun that is made, every warship launched, every rocket fired signifies, in a final sense, a theft from those who hunger and are not fed."[1]

1. *The New York Times*, August 25, 1960.

To contain potential Soviet expansion more cheaply, Eisenhower relied on nuclear weapons. It was less costly, he insisted, to maintain a large stock of nuclear bombs than to arm, feed, clothe, house, and pay millions of soldiers. Nuclear weapons, according to one expression, gave "more bang for the buck." John Foster Dulles, Eisenhower's secretary of state, described how nuclear weapons would do their job *without* being used. The key was to threaten the Soviet Union with "massive retaliation" if it became too aggressive. The threat would be believable if in a crisis the United States practiced "brinkmanship," which meant being prepared to go to the brink of war. As it turned out, brinkmanship proved to be too risky to put into practice, especially after the Soviet Union built up its own nuclear weapons. In reality, the Eisenhower administration tended to be cautious and careful in dealing with the Soviet Union. For example, in 1954 Eisenhower told Syngman Rhee, who wanted U.S. support for a new war to unify Korea: "No one in the world will get us to go to war over these problems. . . . We cannot undertake any engagement that involves [the] deliberate intention of going to war with the Iron Curtain countries."[2]

In effect, then, the main result of Eisenhower's new policy was that it enabled him to keep military spending lower than it had been under Truman.

## KHRUSHCHEV'S "PEACEFUL COEXISTENCE"

If "brinkmanship" turned out to be much less threatening than it sounded, the post-Stalin Soviet foreign policy of "peaceful coexistence" turned out to be less friendly than it sounded.

2. Quoted in Walter LaFaber, *America, Russia, and the Cold War, 1945–1992*, 7th ed. (New York: McGraw-Hill, 1992), p. 156.

Until the 1950s, official Communist doctrine said that war between the capitalist and Communist worlds was inevitable, and that it would lead to the victory of communism. By the 1950s, with both sides armed with growing supplies of nuclear weapons, such a war was clearly suicidal. Under Khrushchev's leadership, therefore, the Soviets adopted the doctrine of peaceful coexistence. Peaceful coexistence did not mean the end of competition between communism and capitalism, or the end of the Cold War. It simply meant that the competition between the two systems would be peaceful. Communism, by providing a better life for its people, would overwhelm and replace capitalism without shooting.

Nor did peaceful coexistence mean that the Soviet Union would not *expand* the area of competition. Khrushchev in fact worked hard to expand Soviet influence in parts of the world previously untouched by the Cold War. The Soviets became active in Asia and Africa, where the old European colonial empires were disintegrating and where anti-Western sentiment was strong. Eventually Khrushchev turned his attention to the Western Hemisphere, where the United States long had been unchallenged. In other words, peaceful coexistence was a nonviolent way of undermining the United States and the West. As a result, it did little to end the Cold War, and often had the opposite effect.

Nikita Khrushchev at the United Nations in 1960. The Soviet leader's policy of "peaceful coexistence" didn't prevent him from leveling sharp words at the West.

The Soviet Union's need to reduce international tensions led to several agreements that temporarily improved Soviet-American relations and produced a short thaw in the Cold War. The first was the armistice that ended the Korean War. A year later another Asian war, this one in Southeast Asia, was brought to an end. Since 1946, France had been fighting a war against Communist-led rebels in its colony of Vietnam. The Communists, known as the Vietminh and skillfully led by Ho Chi Minh, controlled large parts of Vietnam, especially in the northern part of the country. With Soviet cooperation, a conference in Geneva produced an agreement known as the Geneva Accords, under which the French agreed to leave Vietnam. The country itself was divided at the 17th parallel, with the Communists controlling the north and the French and their non-Communist Vietnamese allies in charge in the south. The division was supposed to be temporary; nation-wide elections were to be held in 1956 to unite the country.

However, the United States feared that the Communists might win, in part by manipulating the elections in the areas they controlled, and would use whatever methods they could to take over the entire country. As in Korea the great shadow of the People's Republic of China loomed over the landscape. President Eisenhower summed up the U.S. attitude just before the Geneva Conference began:

> *First of all, you have the specific value of a locality in its production of materials that the world needs.*
>
> *Then you have the possibility that many human beings pass under the control of a dictatorship that is inimical to the free world.*
>
> *Finally, you have . . . what you would call the "falling domino" principle. You have a row of*

*dominos set up, you knock over the first one, and what will happen to the last one is the certainty that it will go over very quickly.*[3]

According to this "domino theory," it was essential to prevent Communists from taking power in Vietnam, or all the other countries of Southeast Asia would fall as well. To prevent the Vietnam domino from falling, the United States sent aid to an anti-Communist Vietnamese faction in the south led by a nationalist named Ngo Dinh Diem. With U.S. help, Diem organized the government of South Vietnam. Across the 17th parallel was Communist North Vietnam. The Cold War had divided yet another country, setting the stage for a conflict that would last much longer than the war in Korea and cost the United States far more in money, prestige, and lives.

Elsewhere in the world, the post-1953 thaw produced more lasting solutions. After World War II, Austria, like Germany, had been divided into four occupation zones. In May of 1955 the Soviets agreed to withdraw from their zone and permit Austrian reunification, provided Austria remain neutral in the Cold War. The Soviets also withdrew from a naval base they had occupied in Finland, a country that before 1918 had been part of the old Russian Empire. Shortly thereafter the first postwar summit meeting between the leaders of the United States, the Soviet Union, Great Britain, and France took place in Geneva. The meeting in effect marked the international debut of Nikita Khrushchev as his country's leader. However, despite talk about a new and friendlier "Spirit of Geneva," nothing concrete was accomplished.

3. News Conference, April 7, 1954, *Public Papers of the Presidents, Dwight D. Eisenhower, 1954* (Washington, D.C.: U.S. Government Printing Office, 1960), pp. 282–283.

## 1956: FROM EASTERN EUROPE
## TO THE SUEZ CANAL

The first thaw in the Cold War lasted until 1956. It ended as a result of two crises that took place almost simultaneously, one in Eastern Europe and the other in the Middle East.

The crisis in Eastern Europe developed in October when a revolt against Soviet control broke out in Hungary. Because some American officials, particularly Secretary of State Dulles, had said they hoped to "liberate" Eastern Europe, the Hungarians hoped the United States would intervene to help them. However, the United States had no intention of risking a world war over Eastern Europe. It did nothing as Soviet troops and tanks brutally crushed the revolt early in November. Over 20,000 Hungarians died, while over 200,000 of their luckier countrymen managed to escape to the West. A final message from Hungary before the revolt's defeat only added to the bitterness and frustration felt by millions of Americans: "Help!—help!—help!—SOS—SOS—SOS! They just brought us a rumor that the American troops will be here within one or two hours. . . . We are well and fighting."[4]

While the revolution in Hungary was worsening Cold War relations in Europe, warfare in the Middle East added to the tensions. Many streams of hostility flowed together to cause the Suez Crisis of 1956. Egypt, through whose territory the Suez Canal runs, was led by a dictator named Gamal Abdel Nasser, who dreamed of becoming leader of the entire Arab world. Nasser also dreamed of building a great hydroelectric dam on the Nile River to increase his country's farmland and provide it with electricity. He

4. Quoted in Stephen E. Ambrose, *Rise to Globalism: American Foreign Policy Since 1938*, 6th rev. ed. (New York: Penguin Books, 1991), p. 252.

Hungarian rebels take aim at members of the
secret police as civilians look on. Soviet troops
and tanks soon crushed the rebellion.

hoped for U.S. aid in building the dam, but his request was rejected when his government recognized Mao Zedong's Communist regime in China. The United States refused to aid Nasser in part because it felt Nasser was becoming too friendly with Communist nations. To Nasser, however, there was nothing wrong with being friendly with both Communist and capitalist nations, a view shared by many leaders in Asia and Africa. They considered themselves neutral in the Cold War, despite U.S. and Soviet attempts to get them to choose sides.

After the United States refused to build his dam, Nasser took a step that led to war. To raise money for his dam, he seized control of the highly profitable Suez Canal from its owner, Great Britain. This upset not only Britain, but France as well, since both countries imported Middle Eastern oil via the canal. Another country concerned about Nasser's intentions was Egypt's neighbor Israel. Since Israel's founding in 1948, it had been the victim of murderous Arab terrorist attacks, many launched from Egypt, that killed hundreds of Israeli civilians. Furthermore, Egypt was determined to destroy Israel and had maintained a constant state of war with its tiny neighbor.

Britain, France, and Israel therefore joined to attack Egypt at the end of October, right in the middle of the Hungarian crisis. Both the United States and the Soviet Union opposed the attack, but for different reasons. The Soviets used the incident to win friends in the Arab world by threatening military strikes against the British, French, and Israelis. The United States was angry that its NATO allies had acted without consulting Washington. Pressure from the two superpowers forced Britain, France, and Israel to withdraw from Egypt. The main winner in this multifaceted crisis was the Soviet Union. Egypt and most Arab nations were angry at the United States because Britain and France were its allies and because the United States was friendly to Israel. The Soviet Union meanwhile agreed to build Nasser's dam, which increased its influence in Egypt and elsewhere in the Arab world.

Having brought its allies into line, the United States decided that it would have to act on its own to prevent the spread of communism into the oil-rich Middle East. In 1957 the President extended Cold War containment into the region with what was called the Eisenhower Doctrine, which said the United States would use force to prevent Communist takeovers in the region. The next year, the United States sent 14,000 marines to the small country of Lebanon to protect its shaky pro-Western government.

## THE COLD WAR IN THE THIRD WORLD

The term *third world* was coined to refer to the huge portion of the world that was not part of the industrialized Western world (the "first" world) or the Communist bloc (the "second" world). It included much of Asia, all of Africa, and all of Latin America. Prior to the late 1940s, much of Asia and Africa was part of Western colonial empires or very much under Western influence. By the 1950s these empires were disintegrating and dozens of new nations were becoming independent.

These developments turned the third world into yet another Cold War arena. To the United States and its industrialized allies, the nations of the third world were an important source of raw materials and markets. Some could also provide the United States with valuable military bases. To the Soviet Union the third world was an opportunity to expand its influence at the expense of the United States. As early as 1955 Nikita Khrushchev made a tour of several third world nations. Thereafter, the Soviets gave economic and military aid to a number of newly independent third world nations. They were especially successful in winning friends in India, the second most populous country in the world, and in Egypt, the most populous and powerful Arab state. The Soviets also supported rebellions against colonial powers or pro-Western regimes in the third world. They called these armed uprisings—which often produced brutal dictatorships when they succeeded—"wars of national liberation." The most important of these so-called wars of national liberation began around 1960 in South Vietnam, where Soviet-backed Communist guerrillas battled against a U.S.-supported government.

The United States tried to combat Soviet penetration of the third world in several ways. It offered large amounts of foreign aid to non-Communist regimes, although sometimes that aid went to undemocratic regimes whose only selling point was that they were anti-Communist. The United States also sponsored two alliances involving third World countries: the Central Treaty Organization (CENTO) and the Southeast Asia Treaty Organization (SEATO). Most controversial were secret attempts to overthrow pro-Soviet regimes or those regarded as unfriendly to the West. This was done successfully in Iran in 1953 and in Guatemala in 1954.

In Iran the prime minister, Mohammed Mossadegh, had succeeded in pushing aside Iran's shah, or king. Discarding the shah's pro-Western policies, Mossadegh allied himself with a pro-Communist political party and seized control of the British-owned Anglo-Iranian Oil Company. A CIA agent then was sent to Iran, where he helped overthrow Mossadegh and restore the shah to power. In Guatemala, where the government had nationalized American-owned property, the job of organizing the coup went to the U.S. ambassador. First two CIA planes bombed the capital city. Then the ambassador, accompanied by several marines and carrying a pistol, confronted the Guatemalan president and demanded that he resign. That accomplished, the United States installed its choice as president of Guatemala.

Not all U.S.-sponsored coups were as successful as those in Iran and Guatemala. But in the long run, even where such activities succeeded, they almost certainly made the United States more enemies than friends, especially when the secrets became public.

## NUCLEAR WEAPONS AND THE ARMS RACE

Undoubtedly the most harrowing aspect of the Cold War was the nuclear arms race to which it gave birth. The arms race reached a new and far more terrifying level in the early 1950s with the development of the hydrogen, or thermonuclear, bomb. While there were limits on the size of atomic bombs—the Hiroshima bomb was the equivalent of 20,000 tons of TNT—thermonuclear bombs in theory had no limit in size. The United States tested its first deliverable thermonuclear bomb in February 1954, while the Soviets tested theirs in November 1955. The new hydrogen bombs were measured in *millions* of tons of TNT, which made them hundreds of times more powerful than ordinary atomic bombs.

Both sides also developed bombers and missiles to deliver those bombs. During the 1950s the United States had more and better bombers for that purpose. However, in 1957 the Soviet Union tested the world's first intercontinental missile, in other words a missile able to fly from the Soviet Union to the United States. A few months later, in October 1957, the Soviets used one of their huge new rockets to launch the world's first artificial satellite. Called *Sputnik*, that satellite gave the Soviet Union a lead in another race—the space race—a lead it would hold into the 1960s. In 1961, for example, a Soviet, Yuri Gagarin, became the first human to orbit the earth. Nonetheless, by 1960 the United States had more (and more accurate) intercontinental missiles than the Soviet Union. But Americans, no less than Soviet citizens, lived under the constant threat that a nuclear war would cause tens and possibly hundreds of millions of deaths and destroy their country and world as they knew it.

## THE LAST YEARS OF
## THE EISENHOWER ADMINISTRATION

Between 1959 and January 1961, Cold War tensions grew despite efforts to improve Soviet-American relations. In 1959, Nikita Khrushchev accepted President Eisenhower's invitation and became the first Russian or Soviet leader ever to visit the United States. Despite some rough spots where Khrushchev lost his temper in public, the visit was a huge success. The Soviet leader was at his best talking with farmers in Iowa about how to grow corn and visiting with factory workers in Pittsburgh steel mills. One of his angry outbursts was easily understood by millions of American children: For security reasons Khrushchev was denied his request to visit Disneyland. The American explanation did not satisfy Khrushchev, who asked, "Is there an epidemic of cholera there [in Disneyland] or something? Do you have rocket launching pads there? . . . Or have gangsters taken over the place?"5

Khrushchev's televised farewell speech to the American people was much warmer, and genuinely reflected the Soviet leader's feelings. He began his speech in English with the words "Good evening, American friends." Then, in Russian, with an interpreter translating, he went on to say that he liked "your beautiful cities and roads, but most of all your amiable and kindhearted people." His conclusion, again in English, was "Good luck, American

5. Quoted in Bernard A. Weisberger, Cold War, Cold Peace: The United States and Russia Since 1945 (New York: American Heritage, 1984), p. 192.

friends."[6] However, Khrushchev's final meeting with President Eisenhower failed to break any of the many deadlocks between the Soviet Union and the United States.

Meanwhile, major problems continued to build. The Soviets still wanted to get the United States, Britain, and France out of West Berlin. In 1958, Soviet threats failed to push the Western powers out of the city, but tensions remained. The United States for its part was increasingly concerned about Cuba, where a revolution brought Fidel Castro to power in 1959. By 1960 it was clear that Castro was a Communist, and Soviet support for his regime angered the Americans. In May of that year, a scheduled Eisenhower-Khrushchev summit meeting in Paris collapsed over the downing of the U.S. U-2 spy plane over Soviet territory. A furious Khrushchev demanded that Eisenhower apologize for the flight, but the President refused. Khrushchev, who already was in Paris, then left the city and returned to the Soviet Union. In September the Soviet leader was back in the United States, uninvited, for a meeting of the UN General Assembly in New York City. Khrushchev put on one of his worst public performances at the United Nations. His speech violently attacked the then UN secretary-general, Dag Hammarskjold, as well as the United Nations itself. A few days later Khrushchev shocked the Assembly and the world when, during a speech he did not like, he loudly banged his desk with a shoe while shouting at the stunned speaker. In the commotion that followed, the chairman of the meeting broke his gavel as he struggled to restore order. Khrushchev rounded out his New York trip by meeting with Fidel Castro, who also was there for the General Assembly meeting. Their widely photographed mutual admiration succeeded mainly in antagonizing the United States.

6. Louis Halle, *The Cold War as History* (New York: Harper & Row, 1962), p. 366.

As 1960 and Eisenhower's term as president drew to a close, the world waited to see if new leadership in the United States would improve Soviet-American relations. But events already had been set in motion that within two years would lead to the most dangerous crisis of the Cold War.

An Atlas intercontinental ballistic missile (ICBM) roars skyward in a 1963 test firing.

John F. Kennedy is showered with confetti
while campaigning in Los Angeles in 1960.
Kennedy's youthful style energized American
politics, and his election as president
opened a new era in the Cold War.

# SEVEN

## KENNEDY, KHRUSHCHEV, CUBA, AND CASTRO

When John F. Kennedy ran for president in 1960, he sounded a note of alarm. The youthful, handsome, and energetic candidate said he was worried the United States had stagnated under President Eisenhower and was losing the Cold War to the Soviet Union and communism. As he put it:

> I think there is a danger that history will make a judgment that these were the days when the tide began to run out for the United States. These were the times when the communist tide began to pour in.[1]

Kennedy promised the American people that he would get the country "moving again." When he took office in Janu-

1. *The New York Times*, August 25, 1960.

ary 1961, he immediately introduced his own version of containment, called "flexible response." Kennedy's program was based on the idea that under Eisenhower the United States had relied too much on nuclear weapons to contain communism. He pointed out that the United States never would use nuclear weapons if Communist forces threatened to take over a small country in Asia or Africa. Therefore the country had to build up its regular (or "conventional") forces to meet the Communist threat as it existed worldwide. The new president also believed that the United States needed stronger *nonmilitary* weapons to fight the Cold War. This meant foreign economic aid programs like his Alliance for Progress for Latin America and the Food for Peace program to provide immediate need to the hungry. It also meant the Peace Corps, Kennedy's best-known nonmilitary program. By 1963 that program had sent over five thousand young and idealistic Americans to help people in over forty countries improve their lives.

On top of this, Kennedy was convinced that America's nuclear arsenal was inadequate. He worried that the Soviets might destroy U.S. nuclear bombers on the ground during a surprise attack, or shoot them down with their new antiaircraft missiles. Kennedy also wanted the U.S. nuclear strength to be overwhelmingly greater than the Soviet Union's. Both these problems could be solved by speeding the production of nuclear missiles. During 1961, Kennedy therefore doubled the production of land-based intercontinental missiles and increased by fifty percent the production of submarines that could launch nuclear missiles. Ironically, at this time Soviet leader Nikita Khrushchev was looking for a way to limit the number of nuclear missiles each side would build. Khrushchev needed his resources for improving the Soviet standard of living, and therefore wanted to limit the growth of military spending. But Khrushchev's conduct in several instances during 1961 and 1962 was tactless and threatening and only left

Kennedy more convinced than ever of the Soviet threat. The result was increased tension, a growing arms race, and a crisis that brought the world to the brink of nuclear war.

## 1961: FROM CUBA TO VIENNA TO BERLIN

By 1961, U.S.-Cuban relations had sunk to an all-time low. In one of its last acts, the Eisenhower administration had broken diplomatic relations with Cuba, which had moved solidly into the Communist bloc. By then the CIA already had made several of what it later admitted were at least five assassination attempts, all unsuccessful—Castro claimed the actual number was twenty—against the Cuban leader. One plot involved paying the Mafia $150,000 to do the job. In the wake of its inability to kill Castro, the CIA tried another approach. If Castro could not be killed, the CIA reasoned, perhaps he could be embarrassed and thereby undermined. One inventive scheme called for Castro to make a fool of himself after smoking a cigar laced with a hallucinogenic drug. Another called for dusting his shoes with a drug that, once inhaled, would make the Cuban dictator's beard fall out. Presumably Castro's beard, like Samson's hair, was the key to his power, and once shorn of it the Cuban leader, like the biblical warrior, would fall to his enemies.

Meanwhile, Eisenhower also had begun preparing an invasion to overthrow Castro. The invasion would be carried out by anti-Castro Cuban exiles, who would be trained by the United States and given U.S. air and naval support when they went ashore in Cuba.

Kennedy proceeded with Eisenhower's plan. The new American president was especially concerned because Castro clearly wanted to spread his Communist revolution to other Latin American countries. In April 1961 a small anti-Castro force of about 1,500 men landed in Cuba at a

Cuban leader Fidel Castro. As Castro moved
solidly into the Communist bloc, relations with
the United States soured rapidly.

place called the Bay of Pigs. However, although U.S. boats took them to Cuba, Kennedy did not provide them with air cover because he wanted to limit direct U.S. involvement. The invasion was a disaster. The entire anti-Castro force was killed or captured. Kennedy was embarrassed, both because the United States had supported an attack on a small neighbor and because the defeat made him and the United States look incompetent and weak.

Matters soon went from bad to worse. In June, Kennedy went to the Austrian capital of Vienna for a "get acquainted" meeting with Khrushchev. The Soviet leader acted aggressive during the talks and came away from the meeting thinking he could push the young American president around. Kennedy later acknowledged that he had done poorly in Vienna and was determined to show Khrushchev that he could be as tough as any leader. As he told one of his advisers, "If Khrushchev wants to rub my nose in the dirt, it's all over. That son of a bitch won't pay any attention to words. He has to see you move."[2]

In the summer of 1961, however, it was Khrushchev, not Kennedy, who moved. The start of a new decade had not ended the old problems in Berlin. They had, in fact, grown worse, at least from the Soviet point of view. Since 1945 several million East Germans had used Berlin to flee to the West. It was easy because Berlin, while divided politically into East and West, was physically still one city. Any East German could come to East Berlin and take a subway ride to freedom in West Berlin. Once in West Berlin, the new arrival could stay or travel on to the rest of West Germany. This was a serious drain on East Germany, which was losing many of its most talented young people to the West. And by the summer of 1961 the drain had become a flood. Thirty thousand East Germans were pouring

2. Quoted in Arthur M. Schlesinger, *A Thousand Days* (Boston: Houghton Mifflin, 1965), p. 259.

through the Berlin floodgate to the West each month, and with them went the future of the country they had left behind.

On August 13 the Soviet Union moved to plug the hole by building the Berlin Wall. Kennedy and other Western leaders were outraged, but there was little they could do. The Soviets and their East German puppets were building the wall inside East Berlin. An attempt to knock it down could have been considered an act of war. President Kennedy immediately ordered a convoy of soldiers sent from West Germany along one of the normal highway routes to West Berlin. This demonstrated that the United States and its allies still retained their postwar rights to enter and leave West Berlin. But the Soviets had accomplished their main objective: They had sealed off West Berlin as an escape route.

Despite its undeniable success as a barrier, the Berlin Wall was not a total Soviet victory. It could not hide the failure of communism in East Germany when measured against freedom and capitalism in West Germany. About two years after the Wall went up, President Kennedy made that point when he came to West Berlin and made a speech directly in front of the Wall. The President noted that some people believed there was no important difference between freedom and communism. "Let them come to Berlin," he challenged. It was a dramatic and effective statement that echoed through three decades, until the end of the Cold War. But when they were spoken, Kennedy's eloquent words only bounced off the Berlin Wall, whose

---

**Kennedy and Khrushchev in Austria. The Soviet leader left the meeting believing that the young American president was weak.**

shadow, like the Cold War it symbolized, continued to darken the international landscape.

## THE CUBAN MISSILE CRISIS

If the year 1961 gave the Cold War its most famous symbol, October 1962 witnessed its most dangerous crisis. The roots of the crisis that brought the world so terribly close to nuclear war ran to both Washington and Moscow. After the Bay of Pigs fiasco, American hostility toward Cuba intensified. So did U.S. efforts to undermine Castro. As part of what was called Operation Mongoose, CIA agents contaminated Cuban sugar bound for the Soviet Union and carried out other acts of sabotage. Fidel Castro therefore was correct when he said, "If the United States had not been bent on liquidating the Cuban revolution, there would not have been an October crisis."[3] In addition to overall American hostility toward Cuba, President Kennedy—still smarting from his wounds from the Bay of Pigs, Vienna, and the Berlin Wall—was determined not to appear weak the next time he and Nikita Khrushchev met in diplomatic combat.

In Moscow, Khrushchev had worries of his own that were far more serious than Kennedy's. Several of Khrushchev's economic programs were in trouble, including an ambitious effort to grow grain in semiarid Asian regions of the Soviet Union. Soviet production of intercontinental nuclear missiles lagged behind that of the United States. In 1961 the American advantage was more than two-to-one, and Khrushchev was under pressure from powerful forces within the Communist party to spend more on the military. Khrushchev also ran into trouble when he attempted re-

3. Quoted in Frank Mankiewicz and Kirby Jones, *With Fidel: A Portrait of Castro and Cuba* (New York: Ballantine Books, 1975), p. 150.

forms in other areas, such as culture and the arts. Conservative leaders in the Communist party feared that Khrushchev's more open policies would undermine the party's power. In addition, pressure from abroad hurt Khrushchev. China, the other Communist giant, was bitterly critical of both Khrushchev's reforms at home and his attempts to improve relations with the United States.

In short, Khrushchev needed to demonstrate that he could improve life in the Soviet Union without neglecting its military might and without being "soft" on the United States. Cuba provided that opportunity. In the spring of 1962 he came up with what he thought was a brilliant idea: He would put a small number of Soviet nuclear missiles in Cuba. This would kill two important birds with one stone, something Khrushchev, who never seemed to have enough resources to do what he wanted, was always trying to do.

First and foremost, the Soviet missiles could threaten the United States from only 90 miles (145 kilometers) away. This would enable the Soviets to partially close the gap with the United States in the nuclear arms race in one stroke, while giving them time to develop more modern intercontinental missiles.

Second, the nuclear missiles would protect Cuba from another American invasion. This was immensely important to the Soviet Union, since Cuba gave them an invaluable base in the Americas. Ironically, while both the Cubans and the Soviets sincerely expected a second American-sponsored invasion of Cuba, in fact the Kennedy administration had no such plans.

The Soviet Union would benefit in a third way if it could install its missiles in Cuba, although this benefit was more symbolic than substantial. The United States had installed nuclear missiles right next door to the Soviet Union in Turkey; putting missiles in Cuba, as Khrushchev put it, would give the Americans "some of their own medicine."

Khrushchev reached his decision to send missiles to Cuba in the spring of 1962, after consulting only a few advisers. The Soviets then asked Castro if he would accept the missiles. The Cuban dictator agreed, although not with great enthusiasm since he understood the United States would be infuriated when it became aware of the Soviet weapons. The plan called for secretly shipping the missiles to Cuba and installing them before the United States spotted them. Khrushchev and his advisers never seriously considered what they would do if the Americans discovered the missiles before they were set up and ready to be fired. Apparently Khrushchev believed that he could again get the better of the inexperienced American leader. Kennedy, Khrushchev told some close advisers, could be taken advantage of because he was "too young, too intelligent, and too weak."[4]

Khrushchev's failure to consider a potential American reaction and what he would do if the missiles were discovered was inexcusably reckless. Making matters worse, no serious attempts were made to hide the missiles once they arrived in Cuba. They lay out in the open near their launching sites, as ship after ship continued to unload supplies under the gaze of U.S. spy planes. Nor, for that matter, did the Soviets try to disguise the thousands of soldiers they were sending along with the missiles to an island so close to American shores.

The crisis that one Kennedy adviser called the "Gettysburg" of the Cold War, and which Nikita Khrushchev said was a time when "the smell of burning hung in the air," began on October 14, 1962. On that day an American U-2 spy plane, the same kind of aircraft the Soviets had shot down in 1960, photographed Soviet missile sites in Cuba. The photographs showed that the Soviets were

4. Quoted in William G. Hyland, *The Cold War: Fifty Years of Conflict* (New York: Random House, 1991), p. 130.

building forty-two missile launching pads for intermediate range missiles capable of reaching the United States. The launching sites were still incomplete, but the photographs showed they would be ready in a matter of a few weeks. The American pictures revealed that about two dozen missiles already were in Cuba.

Other U.S. estimates about Soviet military strength in Cuba were far less accurate. United States intelligence thought that 10,000 Soviet troops were in Cuba. The actual figure was over 40,000. Nor was the United States aware that Soviet forces in Cuba already had thirty-six nuclear *warheads* for their missiles. And perhaps most dangerous of all, the United States did not know that there were nine short-range, or "tactical," nuclear-tipped missiles in Cuba, ready for use against any troops the United States might send against Cuban and Soviet forces. The presence of these weapons and the U.S. lack of knowledge about them was enormously important. It meant that while the United States and Soviet Union knew they stood on the brink of nuclear war, they did not know that in fact they were standing with one foot already hanging over the edge.

On October 16 the photographs of the Soviet missiles were shown to President Kennedy. That meeting began thirteen days of what quickly became unbearable tension. Kennedy began by assembling a committee of his top advisers. It was called the "Executive Committee," or "Ex Comm." At first the Ex Comm seemed to favor a massive air strike against the missile sites to try to wipe them all out. However, Air Force generals who favored the strike could not guarantee they could wipe out all the missiles, since it was impossible to know if some were hidden away. In addition, an air strike would kill not only Cubans but undoubtedly Soviet military personnel as well. Another objection to a surprise attack came from Robert Kennedy, the President's younger brother and closest adviser. He sent a note to the President that said simply: "I know how

Tojo [the Japanese leader when Japan bombed Pearl Harbor in 1941] felt when he was planning Pearl Harbor."[5] In other words, Robert Kennedy was warning his brother that he risked going down in history as a leader who started a disastrous war with a surprise attack if he launched an attack on Cuba without first trying to end the crisis by less drastic means.

In the end, President Kennedy chose a less extreme option: a naval blockade of Cuba. All ships bound for Cuba would be boarded and searched for weapons before being allowed to proceed to the island. Kennedy announced his decision to the country and the world in a television speech on October 22. It was a grim message, one that did not try to hide the dangers of challenging Khrushchev's brash step. But, as he told the American people, Kennedy believed he had no choice:

> *My fellow citizens, let no one doubt that this is a difficult and dangerous effort on which we have set out. No one can foresee precisely what course it will take or what costs or casualties will be incurred. Many months of sacrifice and self-discipline lie ahead—months in which both our patience and will will be tested, months in which many threats and denunciations will keep us aware of our dangers. But the greatest danger would be to do nothing.[6]*

Aside from proclaiming what he called a "quarantine"—to have officially proclaimed a "blockade" would have

---

5. Robert F. Kennedy, *Thirteen Days: A Memoir of the Cuban Missile Crisis* (New York: W. W. Norton, 1969), p. 31.

6. Ibid, p. 71.

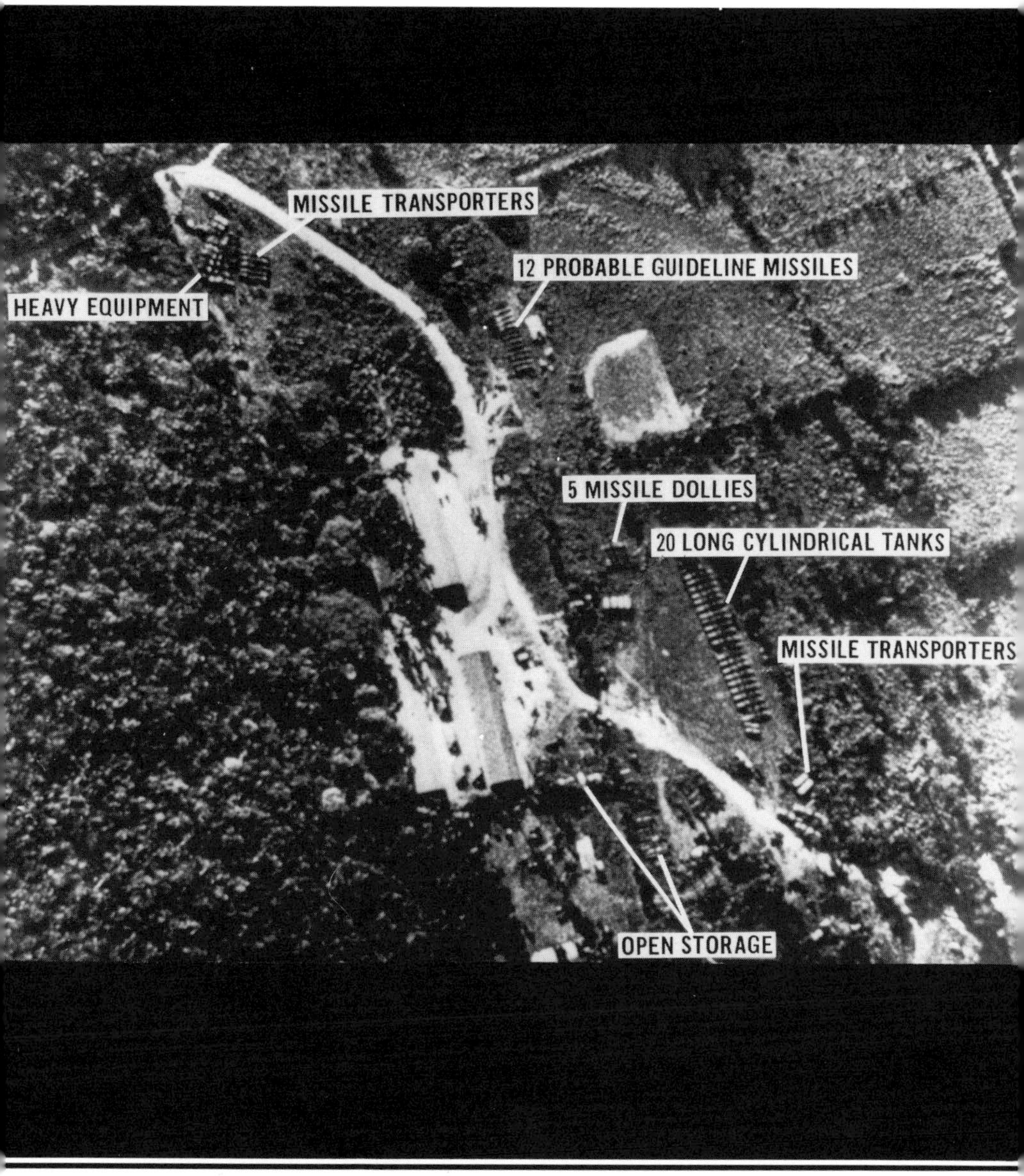
MISSILE TRANSPORTERS
12 PROBABLE GUIDELINE MISSILES
HEAVY EQUIPMENT
5 MISSILE DOLLIES
20 LONG CYLINDRICAL TANKS
MISSILE TRANSPORTERS
OPEN STORAGE

**A photograph taken by an American spy plane in October 1962 shows Soviet missile installations in Cuba.**

legally been an act of war—the President demanded that all Soviet missiles be dismantled and sent home. To back his demands, over 180 naval ships were sent to surround Cuba, and long-range B-52 bombers armed with nuclear bombs took off on patrol. American army units were moved to Florida.

The pressure quickly built as the President and the country waited for the Soviet reaction. Would the Soviets try to finish their missile bases? If so, what would the United States do as the bases neared completion? Would ships honor the U.S. blockade? Or would Soviet warships try to escort cargo ships through it? And how would the United States deal with a Soviet ship that tried to run the blockade? It was clear that a wrong answer to any one of these questions could lead to nuclear war. Robert Kennedy described how the tension affected his brother and himself as they waited to see if the Soviet ships approaching Cuba would try to run the U.S. blockade:

> *Was the world on the brink of a holocaust? Was it our error? A mistake? Was there something further that should have been done? Or not done? His [President Kennedy's] hand went up to his face and covered his mouth. He opened and closed his fist. His face seemed drawn, his eyes pained, almost gray. We stared at each other across the table. For a few seconds it was as though no one else was there and he was no longer the President.*
>
> *Inexplicably, I thought of when he was ill and almost died; when he lost his child; when we learned that our oldest brother had been killed; of personal times of strain and hurt. The voices droned on, but I didn't seem to hear anything. . . .*[7]

7. Ibid., pp. 69–70.

The next few days brought the tension to the breaking point. On the night of October 24–25 several Soviet ships stopped short of the American blockade and turned around. However, other ships continued toward Cuba. The first Soviet offer to try to settle the crisis, a long emotional letter from Khrushchev to Kennedy, arrived on October 26. Along with stating his terms for settling the crisis, Khrushchev stressed that he well understood the catastrophe nuclear war would bring and that he was determined to avoid such a war:

> *You can regard us with distrust, but in any case you can be perfectly sanguine . . . that we are of sound mind and understand perfectly well that if we attack you, you will respond in the same way. . . . This shows that we are normal people, that we understand and evaluate the situation correctly. Therefore how can we permit the incorrect actions which you ascribe to us? Only lunatics or suicides, who themselves want to perish and destroy the whole world before they die, could do this. We, however, want to live and do not at all want to destroy your country. . . .*
>
> *If you have not lost your self-control and sensibly conceive what this might lead to, Mr. President, we and you ought not now to pull on the ends of the rope in which you have tied the knot of war, because the more the two of us pull, the tighter the knot will be tied. And a moment may come when the knot will be tied so tight that not even he who tied it will have the strength to untie it. . . . Let us now take measures to untie the knot.[8]*

8. Quoted in Michael R. Beschloss, *The Crisis Years: Kennedy and Khrushchev, 1960–1963* (New York: Edward Burlingame Books, 1991), pp. 517–520.

However, powerful forces often beyond the control of either Kennedy or Khrushchev were pulling the knot tighter. An American U-2 aircraft checking for radiation from Soviet nuclear tests lost its way and strayed over Soviet territory. It was escorted home by U.S. warplanes that also crossed into Soviet territory before coming home. On October 27 a U-2 was shot down over Cuba and the pilot killed. The U.S. secretary of defense, Robert McNamara, was shocked to find an American warship cruising in the wrong area and the admiral in charge unable to explain why. Even more dangerous, U.S. warships forced Soviet submarines to surface *before* the President told them to do so. And on October 27, Fidel Castro sent Khrushchev a telegram in which he urged "the immediate launching of a nuclear strike on the United States."[9] Khrushchev meanwhile had sent Kennedy a second letter, this one demanding more concessions from the United States in exchange for withdrawing the Soviet missiles.

While all this was going on, Soviet forces in Cuba had received permission to use their nine tactical nuclear warheads against invading American troops. Had the United States sent an invasion force, which it was very close to doing, its soldiers would have been wiped out on the beach by these small nuclear weapons. Secretary McNamara had suggested what would have happened next:

> *Although the U.S. forces would not have been accompanied by tactical nuclear warheads, no one should believe that had U.S. troops been attacked with nuclear warheads, the U.S. would have refrained from responding with nuclear warheads. Where would it have ended? In utter disaster.*[10]

9. Fedor Burlatsky in *The New York Times*, October 23, 1992.

10. *The New York Times*, October 14, 1992.

In the end, Kennedy offered to resolve the crisis on the basis of Khrushchev's *first* letter of October 26. The final agreement was reached on October 28, thirteen days after Kennedy had been told Soviet missiles were in Cuba. The Soviet Union removed its missiles from Cuba in return for a public U.S. pledge not to invade Castro's island. In addition, the United States secretly agreed to remove its missiles from Turkey, a step Kennedy actually had ordered before the Cuban crisis because the Turkish missiles were obsolete.

The Cold War's Gettysburg had not led to gunfire. The men who stepped back from the brink in the nick of time now had the chance to learn something from their brush with catastrophe.

## THE LAST YEARS OF
## KENNEDY AND KHRUSHCHEV

It is difficult to pick a winner in the Cuban Missile Crisis; in fact, it is probably fairer to say that both sides won since war was avoided. Kennedy got the Soviet missiles out of Cuba, but the Castro regime was now safe from a U.S. invasion and the Cubans continued to serve Soviet interests worldwide until the end of the Cold War. More important, both President Kennedy and Premier Khrushchev reacted to the Cuban Missile Crisis by trying to lessen Cold War tensions. The first step was to install a "hot line" communications network between the Kremlin and the White House. That would allow the leaders of the two superpowers to communicate immediately and directly in any future crisis. In July 1963 the two nations signed a treaty that outlawed nuclear tests in the atmosphere. In the future the Soviets and Americans would conduct their nuclear tests underground. This important treaty greatly reduced the fallout from nuclear tests, which can cause cancer and other serious health problems. Unfortunately, several nations that were just developing nuclear weapons, including France and the People's Republic of China, continued to test nuclear weapons above ground.

Had Kennedy and Khrushchev remained in office, it is quite possible that additional steps would have been taken to further defuse the Cold War. However, President Kennedy was assassinated on November 22, 1963. Khrushchev, while safe from any physical attacks, was politically wounded by the Cuban Missile Crisis and never recovered his strength. His hard-line opponents in the Soviet Union were furious. They blamed him for allowing the United States to forge ahead in the race to build intercontinental nuclear missiles. They also blamed him for allowing the Soviet Union to be humiliated when it was forced to remove its missiles from Cuba. In October 1964, further weakened by problems at home, Khrushchev was removed from office. He died in 1971.

By then the focus of the Cold War had shifted. Both the Soviet Union and the United States had built so many nuclear weapons that both sides, realizing that they were less secure than ever, were seriously looking for ways to control the arms race. And instead of Cuba, the country that dominated the news of the Cold War from the mid-1960s to the mid-1970s was a small divided nation in Southeast Asia, Vietnam.

# EIGHT

## VIETNAM

The war in Vietnam was the opposite of the Cuban Missile Crisis. The Missile Crisis exploded suddenly and lasted barely two weeks. The Vietnam War developed gradually and, in its various forms, lasted for over a decade. The Missile Crisis focused on an island in the Caribbean Sea just off the southern tip of the United States. The Vietnam War was fought in a small country in Southeast Asia, 10,000 miles (16,000 kilometers) from American shores. During the Missile Crisis most Americans rallied around their president. During the Vietnam War millions of Americans turned against the president, and the country ended up more divided than at any time since the Civil War. The Missile Crisis was almost bloodless; the only official American death was that of the pilot whose U-2 spy plane was shot down. The Vietnam War cost several million lives, including those of over 58,000 American soldiers. After the Cuban Missile Crisis both sides could claim some sort of victory, although the United States generally was viewed as the overall winner. The Vietnam War ended in defeat for the United States and in the destruction of South Vietnam, the non-Communist country the United States was trying to preserve.

The Vietnam War was the single most dramatic and costly example of the expansion of the Cold War to the third world. After the Communist victories in China and North Vietnam and the stalemate in Korea, the United States intensified its efforts to stop the further spread of communism in Asia. One country that seemed particularly vulnerable to Communist pressure was South Vietnam. Part of the problem was that the South Vietnamese government under Ngo Dinh Diem was dictatorial and corrupt. In addition, Diem and many of the key officials in his government were Roman Catholics who ruled a land overwhelmingly made up of Buddhist peasant farmers. The Diem regime did nothing to help the majority of the peasants, who did not have enough land, and Diem added to his problems by treating the Buddhist majority poorly. His policies soon led to opposition and eventually to open revolt.

All of this played into the hands of Communist forces in Vietnam. Ho Chi Minh's Communist regime in the north was a dictatorship that was both stronger and more brutal than Diem's in the south. It took advantage of Diem's troubles by sending help to the rebels in the south, and it soon took over the anti-Diem uprising. In 1960 an organization called the National Liberation Front (NLF) was set up in South Vietnam to run the rebellion. Although the NLF contained non-Communists, it was led and controlled by Communists loyal to Ho. Diem referred to the organization as Vietnamese Communists, or Vietcong, a name that stuck. By 1961 the Vietcong already were threatening to defeat Diem and take over South Vietnam.

## KENNEDY AND VIETNAM: 1961–1963

When Kennedy became president, the United States was sending limited amounts of economic and military aid to the Diem regime. There also were about three thousand U.S. military advisers in the country to help the South Vietnamese Army. Kennedy believed that this was not enough, and he was determined to keep South Vietnam from going Communist.

Kennedy's view of the Vietnam situation, which followed the logic of the U.S. policy of containment, assumed that Moscow and Beijing were the real source of the trouble in Vietnam. The U.S. government also assumed that Communist uprisings anywhere in the third world could be traced to the Soviet Union or China, the world's Communist giants. In other words, a Communist victory in Vietnam would be a defeat for non-Communists that would spread far beyond South Vietnam. This was what Kennedy's top advisers told him shortly after he took office:

*The loss of South Vietnam would make pointless any further discussion about the importance of Southeast Asia to the free world; we would have to face the near certainty that the remainder of Southeast Asia and Indonesia would move to a complete accommodation with Communism, if not formal incorporation with the Communist bloc.*[1]

As far as the struggle inside South Vietnam was concerned, the United States believed that the Communist forces in the south took their orders directly from Ho Chi Minh's government in the north.

1. "1961 Rusk-McNamara Report to Kennedy on South Vietnam," in *The Pentagon Papers* (New York: Bantam Books for *The New York Times*, 1971), p. 150.

Only part of this analysis was accurate. By the early 1960s there was no unified Communist world. The Soviet Union and the People's Republic of China were quarreling, and North Vietnam was independent of both of them. The Vietnamese, Communist or anti-Communist, disliked and feared the Chinese, against whom their country had struggled for its independence for a thousand years. Ho Chi Minh saw the Chinese as a greater long-term threat to his country than the United States was, despite the fact that China was a Communist state and the United States the leader of the world's capitalist states.

What was true about American assumptions about Vietnam was that the Communist uprising in South Vietnam was controlled and directed by North Vietnam. Nonetheless, it was poor local conditions and the repressive policies of the South Vietnamese regime that caused the uprising in the first place.

Under Kennedy, U.S. aid to the South Vietnamese government grew dramatically. By 1963 there were 16,000 U.S. advisers in South Vietnam. Despite the presence of these advisers, Communist guerrillas using hit-and-run tactics continued to be successful against the South Vietnamese. The Communists were helped because the Diem government continued to ignore peasant needs and Buddhist complaints of discrimination. This drove more people, including some non-Communists, to support the rebellion.

By 1963 Kennedy had decided that Diem had to go. The United States therefore secretly let it be known that it would not object if the South Vietnamese Army overthrew Diem. However, Kennedy was shocked when in November 1963 plotters murdered Diem and several members of his family. Three weeks later President Kennedy himself was assassinated. Vice President Lyndon Johnson became president, and a new and painful era of U.S. involvement in Vietnam began.

## JOHNSON AND THE AMERICANIZATION
## OF THE VIETNAM WAR

By 1964 the Vietcong, aided by units of the North Vietnamese Army that had infiltrated into the south, were on the verge of defeating the South Vietnamese. Not even U.S. air power, which was used to bomb Communist forces in the south, could stop their string of victories. It was becoming clearer that U.S. ground forces—not advisers but army units fighting in the field—would be required to stop the Communists. This was something few people wanted to see. American soldiers serving as advisers already had been killed in Vietnam, but if U.S. army units went into battle American casualties would soar.

The stage for direct U.S. intervention in the ground fighting was set during the summer of 1964. On August 2, North Vietnamese gunboats fired on a U.S. destroyer on an intelligence patrol in the Gulf of Tonkin off North Vietnam. A second North Vietnamese attack was reported on August 21, although it is doubtful that attack took place. President Johnson then asked Congress for authority to aid South Vietnam and defend U.S. forces already in the region. On August 7, Congress passed the Gulf of Tonkin resolution. It gave Johnson the authority to "take all necessary measures to repel armed attack against the forces of the United States and to prevent further aggression." The resolution gave the President enormous power. In effect, it allowed him to go to war in South Vietnam without asking Congress for a declaration of war as the U.S. Constitution requires. Or, as Johnson himself put it, the resolution was "like grandma's shirt—it covered everything."[2]

Johnson's policy of escalation—sending more and more troops to South Vietnam and increasing the use of

2. Quoted in Stanley Karnow, *Vietnam: A History* (New York: Viking, 1983), p. 374.

American paratroopers, under attack,
sprint across a field in Vietnam.

U.S. air power in both the south and the north—began in early 1965. By the end of the year over 185,000 U.S. combat troops were in South Vietnam. The number more than doubled in 1966, reached 485,000 in 1967, and hit 535,000 in 1968. Casualties rose as well. In 1965, 1,369 American soldiers died in battle. Over 5,000 died in 1966, over 9,000 in 1967, and over 14,000 in 1968. In addition, hundreds of U.S. soldiers were taken prisoner, especially crews of airplanes shot down in bombing raids over North Vietnam.

Despite the enormous effort and the high price it was paying, the United States was unable to defeat the Communists in South Vietnam. The North Vietnamese and Vietcong proved to be tough and resourceful enemies. Troop reinforcements and supplies from North Vietnam continually flowed into the south along a network of jungle trails called the Ho Chi Minh Trail. They more than replaced the losses suffered in battle. Intensive U.S. bombing of the trail had little effect on the military traffic moving southward. The United States also bombed North Vietnam to force its government to accept U.S. peace terms that would have left a non-Communist government in South Vietnam. But the North Vietnamese were willing to accept the terrible losses the bombing caused, and refused to give in. They also received crucial help in the form of massive shipments of military aid from the Soviet Union, as well as lesser amounts from China.

Meanwhile, enormous shipments of U.S. aid failed to solve the problems of the South Vietnamese government. Its support among the peasant and Buddhist majority remained low, and its army, plagued by low morale and corruption, rarely was a match for the North Vietnamese or Vietcong.

Another frustration for American soldiers was fighting in a country where the enemy hid in the jungle or among a local population that often was unfriendly. American troops could never be sure where the enemy was. And as U.S. casualties mounted without clear signs that the war was being won, many Americans began to turn against the war. Large demonstrations against the war embarrassed the Johnson administration and undermined the war effort. By 1968 the United States was a badly divided country involved in a costly war it seemed unable to win.

## RICHARD NIXON, VIETNAMIZATION, AND THE END OF THE WAR

The presidential election campaign of 1968 was filled with angry demonstrations that showed how divided the United States was over its role in Vietnam. After winning the election by a razor-thin margin, President Richard Nixon reversed Johnson's policy of escalation. He began to withdraw U.S. ground troops from South Vietnam, and American casualties began to fall. The job of fighting the Communists increasingly was turned over to the South Vietnamese Army, a program Nixon called "Vietnamization." To back up the South Vietnamese, Nixon intensified the air war, especially over North Vietnam. He also ordered the secret bombing of neighboring Cambodia and Laos, where Communist forces often took refuge. The President still hoped to force the North Vietnamese to accept an anti-Communist government in the south. He also hoped to convince the Soviet Union to put pressure on the North Vietnamese to accept American peace terms.

Nixon wanted to end the war for two reasons. By 1969 the United States was so bitterly divided that it was impossible to carry on a war. In addition, the President worried that continued involvement in Vietnam was weakening the United States and distracting him from the more important tasks of dealing with the Soviet Union and the PRC. But Nixon's attempts to end the war on favorable terms failed. The Soviets, despite their desire to improve relations with

Opposition to the war mounted in
the United States. Here, members of a
group called Women's Strike for Peace
demonstrate in 1967.

the United States, continued to back the North Vietnamese. With American troops pulling out of South Vietnam, the Communists realized they could outwait the United States. Finally, after four years of negotiations, an agreement was reached in January 1973. There would be a cease-fire, the U.S. would withdraw the remainder of its forces from Vietnam, and all U.S. prisoners in Communist hands would be released. Although the fighting in Vietnam continued, for the United States the longest war in its history, and its least successful, was finally over.

## RESULTS OF THE VIETNAM WAR

Within two years of America's withdrawal from Vietnam, the Vietcong and North Vietnamese overran South Vietnam. The country was unified under the Communist dictatorship that ruled from Hanoi, the North Vietnamese capital, which now became the capital of the entire country. Communist forces also seized power in Cambodia and Laos, Vietnam's two small neighbors to the west.

The Communist victory did not bring peace or prosperity to Vietnam. In 1978 Vietnam invaded neighboring Cambodia, where the new Communist regime was friendly to China but unfriendly to Vietnam. The Vietnamese ousted that regime, the murderous Khmer Rouge, who in just three years had killed at least one million people in a country of seven million. However, to keep the Khmer Rouge out of power, the Vietnamese became bogged down in a struggle that lasted for over a decade. And in 1979 Vietnam was attacked by China in retaliation for its Cambodian invasion. That produced a short but ferocious war. In short, American fears of the expansion of some sort of unified Communist movement were misplaced. Instead, as soon as the United States left Southeast Asia, the Communist states there, without a common enemy to unite them, started fighting each other. The Cold War struggle between the United States and communism was replaced by two hot wars among the Communists themselves.

At the global level, the end of the Vietnam War saw a more restrained United States and a more aggressive Soviet Union. For several years the United States was less willing to get involved in new third world conflicts. Because this reluctance clearly was a reaction to the disastrous Vietnam experience, it was called the "Vietnam Syndrome." The Soviets took advantage of this American inertia to help several Marxist movements come to power, including a pro-Soviet regime in the African country of Angola and in Nicaragua in Central America.

However, despite the damage and upheaval the Vietnam War caused, neither the Soviet Union nor the United States let the war get in the way of bettering relations between themselves. Since the Cuban Missile Crisis, the superpowers had been edging away from the nuclear brink. They continued in that direction as Johnson succeeded Kennedy, and Nixon succeeded Johnson in the United States, and as Leonid Brezhnev succeeded Khrushchev in the Soviet Union. Even as the Vietnam War raged, this movement reduced the intensity of the Cold War and produced its first major agreement for controlling nuclear arms. When it came to nuclear weapons, not even a shooting war could dull the instinct for survival.

Kosygin and Johnson at Glassboro,
New Jersey, in 1967.

# NINE

## THE RISE AND FALL
## OF DÉTENTE

In June of 1967, while he was in the middle of escalating the Vietnam War, Lyndon Johnson took a trip to the small town of Glassboro, New Jersey, to meet with Premier Alexei Kosygin, who stood second only to Leonid Brezhnev among Soviet leaders. The meeting did not take place under the best of circumstances. The Vietnam War was increasing tension between the Soviet Union and the United States, and Kosygin, who was in New York City to attend a UN meeting, had refused to come to Washington to meet with Johnson. So the American president, literally meeting Kosygin halfway, traveled north from Washington to Glassboro, while Kosygin traveled south from New York to the New Jersey college town.

The two leaders did not meet to discuss Vietnam, the issue that dominated the headlines at the time. They focused instead on an older and more dangerous problem, the nuclear arms race between their countries. Their goal was to put some kind of limits on that race, which was becoming both increasingly dangerous and expensive. The negotiations designed to accomplish this were known as SALT (Strategic Arms Limitation Talks).

These talks were fated not to get off the ground during Johnson's presidency. In August of 1968 (just two months after the Glassboro meeting) the Soviet Union, assisted by most of its Warsaw Pact satellites, invaded Czechoslovakia, another member of that pact. Czechoslovakia's Communist government had introduced democratic reforms the Soviets believed threatened Communist rule not only in Czechoslovakia but potentially in the rest of their Eastern European empire. Despite protests from the United States and its allies, the Soviets poured 500,000 soldiers into Czechoslovakia. They removed the Czechoslovak government and installed hard-line leaders who revoked the reforms. A month after the invasion, the Soviets announced what came to be called the Brezhnev Doctrine, which bluntly said the Soviet Union would use force if necessary to prevent any changes in Eastern Europe that threatened Communist control there. The invasion of Czechoslovakia temporarily soured Soviet-American relations and ended the SALT talks, but not for long. Both superpowers were committed to improving their relationship. In 1969, with the newly elected Richard Nixon in the White House, the SALT talks resumed. Three years later, after difficult negotiations, they finally produced the first arms control treaty of the Cold War.

## THE ORIGINS OF DÉTENTE

The improved Soviet-American relationship that made the SALT talks possible, and which those talks in turn helped foster, was known as "détente," a French word that means

**Soviet tanks line a street in Prague,
Czechoslovakia, in 1968.**

"the relaxation of tensions." Détente, which lasted from the late 1960s through the mid-1970s, did not end the Soviet-American rivalry. Nor did it prevent a deterioration of Soviet-American relations later on. But it led to many important and lasting agreements and increased ties between the governments of the two countries, and between their citizens as well. Détente also was, in effect, an admission by both sides that they had to take serious steps to create a more stable world. It therefore was a crucial turning point in the Cold War.

The origins of détente lay in the changing problems and needs of the Cold War's two superpowers, as well as the opportunities they saw for themselves if they could ease their Cold War burdens. In Washington, President Nixon and his chief foreign policy adviser, Henry Kissinger, saw the United States living in a changing world that was increasingly difficult to manage. The Soviet Union and the United States, notwithstanding their military power, no longer dominated the world as they did immediately after World War II. By the late 1960s Western Europe and Japan, on the basis of their growing economic strength, had become major power centers in their own right. So had the People's Republic of China, the world's second most powerful Communist state and its most populous country. Nixon and Kissinger believed that these new power centers had to cooperate with the United States and the Soviet Union if major problems all over the world were to be solved, or at least controlled. From the point of view of the United States, this meant different things for different nations. For America's NATO allies, it meant they would have to bear a greater share of the burden of their own defense. As Nixon put it in 1970:

*The United States will participate in the defense and development of allies and friends, but ... America cannot—and will not—conceive* all *the plans, design* all *the programs, execute* all *the deci-sions and undertake* all *the defense of the free nations of the world. We will help where it makes a real difference and is considered in our interest.*[1]

Of course, any scheme involving the world's five power centers first and foremost required improved relations between the United States and the Soviet Union. This was an especially difficult problem because by the end of the 1960s the United States seemed to lack the power to deal with its Communist rival. While America was divided and weakened by its war in Vietnam, the Soviet Union, at least in terms of military power, was growing stronger. What Americans found most menacing was that, after a crash campaign to build nuclear weapons, the Soviet Union had caught up to the United States in that area. By 1969 the Soviets had approximately as many "strategic" nuclear weapons (the long-range guided missiles and bombers with which one superpower could hit the other's territory) as the United States. Although the "mix" of these weapons was not the same—the Soviets had more land-based intercontinental missiles while the United States had more bombers and missiles launched from submarines—it was clear that the Soviets had overcome the gap that had forced them to retreat during the Cuban Missile Crisis only seven years earlier. Making matters worse, the Soviets were continuing to build nuclear weapons, and many experts in the United States, including the President, feared they soon would surpass the United States in nuclear firepower. Either a way had to be found to stop or slow the Soviet buildup, or the United States would face an increasingly expensive arms race that would leave it under the shadow of ever more destructive Soviet weapons.

1. Richard M. Nixon, *Foreign Policy for the 1970s: A New Strategy of Peace* (Washington, D.C.: U.S. Government Printing Office, 1970), p. 2.

The Soviet Union had good reasons of its own to improve relations with the United States. Although they had achieved equality with the United States in strategic nuclear weapons, the Soviets still had a long unfulfilled wish list. They wanted the United States to recognize them as an equal in determining how the world should be ordered. In addition, while accepting the reality of Soviet domination of Eastern Europe, the United States and its allies in Western Europe had never recognized that control as legitimate. The Soviets wanted that recognition. They also wanted to expand trade with the West, mainly so they could import the Western technology and equipment needed to modernize their economy, which continued to lag behind the economies of the Western capitalist world.

Furthermore, the Soviets, like the Americans, feared an expensive new arms race. A new phase in the nuclear arms race was sure to involve two new types of weapons. One was the MIRV, or multiple independently targeted reentry vehicle. More simply put, that meant putting more than one nuclear warhead on each guided missile, so that each missile could hit five, ten, or even twenty different targets. This would radically increase the destructive capability of both superpowers, as well as the nuclear threat under which both lived.

Although there was little chance of avoiding the MIRVs, whose development was well under way in the United States, there was a chance of avoiding the second type of weapon. It was the ABM, or antiballistic missile, a defensive missile capable of shooting down other missiles. Developing the ABM, assuming it could be made to work, would be incredibly expensive at a time when Brezhnev needed resources for the civilian Soviet economy. He also understood that the United States, with its superior technological resources, would have a great advantage over the Soviet Union. The Soviets therefore wanted to avoid at least that new phase of the arms race, which would undermine the progress they had made during the 1960s in catching up to the United States.

SALT negotiations began in 1969 and dragged on for several years. Meanwhile, détente moved ahead in other areas. In 1970 the recently elected West German leader, Willy Brandt, a widely respected statesman who had opposed his country's Nazi regime during World War II, broke the ice in Europe. He negotiated treaties in which West Germany accepted the borders Stalin had drawn after World War II. Aside from the assurances this offered Poland, which had gained former German territory as a result of the war, Brandt in effect had accepted the division of Germany, which acceptance the Soviets had long wanted. In return, Brandt demanded Soviet guarantees on permanent Western access to West Berlin, and the Soviets signed an agreement to this effect in 1971. The next year, West Germany formally recognized East Germany, thereby reducing East-West tensions in Europe even further.

The most noticeable improvement in direct Soviet-American relations during the first years of Nixon's presidency involved increased trade, which more than tripled between 1971 and 1972 alone. When the Soviets suffered a poor grain harvest in 1972, a huge grain deal was negotiated in which they purchased twenty-five percent of the entire U.S. wheat crop. That deal pushed the trade figures even higher, fed millions of Soviet citizens, and helped reduce the United States' trade deficit (imbalance between imports and exports). However, millions of American consumers were shocked and upset when the price of grain at home jumped, raising the price of bread and many other food products. Some people angrily referred to the deal as the "great grain robbery." Still, the Nixon administration continued to encourage additional economic ties with America's great Communist rival, and huge American companies like Pepsi-Cola and the Chase Manhattan Bank made plans to do business and make money in the Soviet Union. As U.S. secretary of commerce Peter G. Peterson explained, the Nixon strategy was to build peace through encouraging trade:

*Our purpose is ... to build in both countries a vested economic interest in the maintenance of an harmonious and enduring relationship. ... If we can create a situation in which the use of military force would jeopardize a mutually profitable relationship, I think it can be argued that our security has been enhanced.*[2]

## SALT I

The centerpiece of détente was the Soviet-American arms limitation agreement signed in May 1972 and known as SALT I. This was not the first nuclear agreement signed by the two superpowers. They already had agreed to a partial nuclear test ban treaty in 1963. In 1968, with détente in its infancy, the two nations joined sixty others in signing the Nuclear Nonproliferation Treaty, which attempted to stop the spread of nuclear weapons to other countries. But never had the two superpowers accepted any restrictions whatsoever on their own nuclear arsenals.

SALT I did exactly that with two accords. The first put strict limits on ABMs, which neither country wanted to build because of the expense involved, but which each feared the other might. These limits were so low—two installations per country—as to render ABMs useless. In

2. Quoted in John Lewis Gaddis, *Russia, the Soviet Union, and the United States: An Interpretive History*, 2d ed. (New York: McGraw-Hill, 1990), p. 276.

Opposition to nuclear arms mounted through the 1960s
and 1970s. These marchers took part in an international
demonstration in New York City in 1978.

effect, each superpower agreed to leave itself defenseless against a nuclear attack, on the theory that under such circumstances neither would attack the other because it would itself be destroyed when the other side retaliated. The other SALT I accord put temporary limits on both land-based intercontinental missiles and submarine-launched missiles, the plan being to reduce those limits later on. SALT I actually left the Soviet Union with more nuclear-tipped missiles than the United States. However, because the United States led in the number of missiles with more than one warhead (MIRVs), it actually had more nuclear warheads than the Soviets, and therefore more destructive power.

SALT I had many critics. They pointed out that the limits it set did nothing to reduce the number of nuclear missiles. Also, SALT did nothing to limit MIRVS. As a result, both countries continued to add warheads—the explosives that do the actual destruction—to their arsenals. Still, SALT I was the first Soviet-American agreement that set any limits at all on the superpowers' nuclear weapons. The agreement was expanded slightly in 1974, when Brezhnev and the new American president, Gerald Ford, signed an agreement that added bombers to the list of weapons covered. Whatever its flaws, the SALT agreement meant that a generation of unlimited arms building had ended, and an era of nuclear arms control had begun.

## THE UNITED STATES AND CHINA

While the United States followed its policy of détente with the Soviet Union, it simultaneously dramatically changed its policy toward the world's other Communist giant, the People's Republic of China. The United States, which since 1949 had refused to extend diplomatic recognition to the PRC, changed its policy for several reasons. By 1969, far from being partners in a world Communist conspiracy as some fearful Americans had claimed in the 1950s, the Soviets and Chinese had become angry antagonists. In March of that year, their troops fought a series of bloody battles along their 3,000-mile (4,800-kilometer) border. Thus, by 1969 the Chinese and the Americans found themselves looking for the same thing: a balance against growing Soviet power. And although it took a while, by the early 1970s they found what they needed in each other.

The once bitter enemies quietly began sending signals of changing attitudes as early as 1969. The first public step in this remarkable turnabout occurred in 1971 when an American table tennis team playing in Japan suddenly was invited to visit China. A few months later, Henry Kissinger made a secret visit to Beijing, China's capital. On February 21, 1972, Richard Milhous Nixon, who had become a political star in the late 1940s and early 1950s as one of America's most militant anti-Communists, became the first American president ever to visit China. The scene at the Beijing airport was a far cry from the Geneva Conference of 1954, when American secretary of state John Foster Dulles had refused to shake the hand of Zhou Enlai, China's foreign minister. Now, twenty-eight years later, Zhou was at the airport to greet presidential adviser Kissinger with the words, "Ah, old friend." Not to be outdone, President Nixon, who had taken the trouble to learn how to eat with chopsticks before his trip, responded to a toast at a state dinner by quoting from a poem written by none other than his host, Communist Party Chairman Mao Zedong. As the Communist Mao had written, so the anti-Communist Nixon now spoke, "So many deeds cry out to be done, and always urgently. . . . Seize the day, seize the hour."[3]

3. Quoted in Bernard A. Weisberger, *Cold War, Cold Peace: The United States and Russia Since 1945* (New York: American Heritage, 1984), p. 253.

Although Nixon's trip to Beijing was a spectacular success, many problems remained between the United States and China. The most important involved Taiwan, whose Nationalist government continued to receive U.S. support. It took the United States and China until 1979 to establish full diplomatic relations. Nonetheless, Nixon's trip and overall China policy put additional pressure on the Soviet Union to move toward détente and marked a historic turning point for the better in Chinese-American relations.

## THE HIGH POINT OF DÉTENTE

The high point of détente, both physically and politically, was reached in July 1975. The physical height was reached when U.S. and Soviet spacecraft linked up in space 140 miles (225 kilometers) above the earth. The political height was reached in Helsinki, Finland, at the Conference on Security and Cooperation, attended by the Soviet Union, the United States, Canada, and all the countries of Europe except Albania. The Helsinki Accords signed on August 1 were a great triumph for Leonid Brezhnev and the Soviet Union. The West formally accepted all European borders drawn after World War II, something the Soviets had sought for thirty years. It also agreed to expand trade with the Communist world, which would help the Soviet Union

**Richard Nixon was the first U.S. president to visit China. Here he poses in front of the Great Wall with his wife, Pat, and Chinese and American officials.**

modernize its economy. In exchange, the Soviet Union and its allies agreed to respect the human rights of their citizens.

In 1975 agreeing to respect human rights seemed like a small price to pay for such major Western concessions. The Communist regimes behind the Iron Curtain appeared to have their respective countries under tight control. Nor did the United States and its NATO allies seem inclined to let human rights interfere with détente. They were far more interested in making sure détente relieved them of some of the dangers and costs of the Cold War. However, decay was eating away at communism in both the Soviet Union and its satellites, and discontent was building among their people. In the 1980s the Soviet Union would find that the price it had agreed to pay at Helsinki was much higher than anybody could have imagined.

## THE END OF DÉTENTE
## AND THE "NEW" COLD WAR

Détente did not survive the 1970s. Even during détente, American power was essential to keeping Soviet ambitions under control. However, by the mid-1970s the United States had been weakened by the Vietnam War and the Watergate scandal. Watergate, which occupied and distracted Nixon during 1973 and 1974, finally forced him to resign from office, the only American president ever to do so. It was against that background of American weakness that Leonid Brezhnev and the Soviet leadership made a fateful choice. Instead of restraining their ambitions and reaping the benefits of further reduced Cold War tensions, they followed aggressive policies worldwide. Those policies produced many victims, including détente itself.

The first cracks in the structure of the new Soviet-American relationship appeared as early as 1973, when détente was still in its prime. The cause was a crisis in the Middle East. In October of that year, on the eve of Yom Kippur, the holiest day of the Jewish calendar, the Arab states of Egypt and Syria launched a massive attack against Israel. Both Egypt and Syria had long been friendly to the Soviet Union and were heavily armed with Soviet weapons, while Israel was America's staunchest friend in the Middle East and the only democratic country in the region. In Washington many Americans in Congress and the executive branch were angered that the Soviets had violated the spirit of détente by not warning the United States of the attack. Israel eventually defeated the Arabs with the aid of large emergency U.S. arms shipments, but only after suffering heavy early losses. Meanwhile, the war quickly produced a dangerous Soviet-American confrontation. When the Israelis began to turn the tide of battle, Brezhnev threatened to intervene militarily to help Egypt and Syria. Nixon responded by putting U.S. naval and air forces in the Middle East on alert. However, both superpowers also pressed for a cease-fire, which was arranged after difficult negotiations. The Yom Kippur War and U.S. support of Israel also led to a boycott of oil sales to the United States by the oil-producing Arab states, which damaged the U.S. economy and caused economic hardship to millions of Americans. The Arab oil boycott also weakened the United States in Soviet eyes by demonstrating America's dependence on foreign oil supplies to keep its economy running.

Although détente survived the 1973 Arab-Israeli war, it did not survive Soviet actions after 1975. Part of the problem was that the United States and the Soviet Union had different views of what détente actually meant. The United States believed détente meant restraint and cooperation in a broad range of international issues. The Soviets, on the other hand, considered détente to be limited to specific Soviet-American agreements. They felt free to act as they pleased regarding anything that fell beyond those agreements.

This difference of opinion became clear during the second half of the 1970s. As the United States under President Gerald Ford struggled to recover from the Vietnam War and Watergate, the Soviets took advantage of America's reluctance to get involved in struggles elsewhere in the world. Substantial Soviet support of Communist forces in the African country of Angola, which included the use of Cuban troops, led to a Communist victory there. Soviet-sponsored Cuban troops also moved into Ethiopia to support a Marxist dictatorship that had overthrown the local monarchy. In addition, the Soviet government continued a massive buildup of its conventional forces, while denying to its people the human rights promised under the Helsinki Accords.

Détente was badly damaged but still not entirely dead when Jimmy Carter became president in 1977. Carter came into office determined to go beyond détente and end the Cold War once and for all. One way to do this, he believed, was to focus less on the long-standing Soviet-American confrontation and build an American foreign policy based on new principles. The "soul" of Carter's policy would be human rights. As Carter put it in May of 1977, "It is a new world that calls for a new American foreign policy—a policy based on constant decency in its values and on optimism in our historical vision."[4] However, while promoting human rights was an admirable goal, Carter sometimes was guilty of poor timing when approaching the Soviet Union on the issue. For example, in 1977 he strongly criticized the treatment of human rights activists in the Soviet Union just before he sent Brezhnev a new arms control proposal. This criticism so angered the

4. Quoted in Gaddis, *Russia, the Soviet Union, and the United States*, p. 296.

Cuban troops and Angolan rebels relax after capturing
the seaside town of Ambrizete, Angola, in 1975.
Soviet support of the rebels became a sore point
in relations between the superpowers.

Soviet leadership that they rejected Carter's proposal almost immediately.

Carter's ability to deal with the Soviets also was damaged by events in Iran. In 1977 Carter had called Iran "an island of stability" in the Middle East. But in February 1979 fanatical Islamic fundamentalists led by a cleric, the Ayatollah Ruhollah Khomeini, seized power from the pro-American shah, or king. In November, shortly after the cancer-stricken shah was admitted to the United States for medical treatment, a large mob of Iranians seized the American embassy and took staff members hostage. For the next 444 days, President Carter allowed himself to be consumed by the Iranian hostage crisis. The United States looked like a weak and helpless giant as the Iranians mistreated the hostages and taunted the President. A failed rescue attempt in April 1980 only made Carter look worse. Not until he was about to leave office were the hostages released. By then Carter's foreign policy, and his presidency, lay in ruins.

As the Iranian hostage crisis dragged on, the United States faced a new and disturbing problem. In December 1979 the Soviet Army invaded neighboring Afghanistan. The Soviet goal was to save a pro-Soviet Communist regime that had seized power in 1978. The invasion turned out to be a disaster for the Soviets, who expected a quick victory but found themselves stuck in a costly struggle with Afghan guerrillas.

The immediate impact of the invasion beyond the borders of Afghanistan was to kill détente. President Carter was shocked by the action, which marked the first time since 1945 that the Soviet Army had struck outside the territory of the Soviet Union or its Warsaw Pact allies. During 1980, his last year in office, he took strong measures to punish the Soviets. Carter had just negotiated a new arms control agreement with the Soviets called SALT II. He now withdrew it from consideration by the U.S. Senate, thereby ending any chance of its being put into effect. Carter also restricted trade with the Soviets, including grain sales, and pulled the United States out of the 1980 Olympics, which were to be held in Moscow. Finally, the President announced the "Carter Doctrine," a pledge to use force if necessary to protect the Persian Gulf oil-producing region from Soviet aggression.

By 1981, as Ronald Reagan prepared to enter the White House, all talk of détente or ending the Cold War had ceased. Instead, rumblings were heard about a "new" Cold War. Reagan himself was militantly anti-Soviet. In Moscow anti-American feeling had climbed to a point not seen in years. But the chill of 1980 was not an accurate forecast of the international political weather ahead. After a severe but brief frost, the shifting winds of change brought not a new Cold War but the end of the old Cold War.

Ronald Reagan's speeches, as a candidate
and as president, reflected the renewal
of Cold War tensions in the early 1980s.

# TEN

# WITH A WHIMPER:
# THE END OF THE COLD WAR

When Ronald Reagan was running for president, his campaign speeches echoed the growing fear of the Soviet Union many Americans had as détente crumbled. Some of Reagan's speeches contained Cold War remarks that sounded as if they had been transported, perfectly frozen and preserved, from the frigid 1950s. As he told one audience: "Let's not delude ourselves. The Soviet Union underlies all the unrest that's going on. If they weren't engaged in this game of dominoes, there wouldn't be any hot spots in the world."[1] Reagan went even further after he became president. He warned Americans against "simple-minded appeasement or wishful thinking about our adver-

1. Quoted in Walter LaFaber, *America, Russia, and the Cold War, 1945–1992*, 7th ed. (New York: McGraw-Hill, 1992), p. 304.

saries" and labeled the Soviet Union an "evil empire" that had become "the focus of evil in the modern world."[2]

In Moscow the view of the United States under Reagan's leadership was also grim. One Soviet leader, ignoring the ways his country had provoked the United States in the mid- and late 1970s, said of Reagan: "He offends our national pride. How can we deal with a man who calls us outlaws, criminals, and the source of evil in the world?"[3]

This mistrust of America remained a constant even as the Soviet leadership changed. In November of 1982 Leonid Brezhnev, old and sick after eighteen years in office, died of a heart attack. Brezhnev was succeeded by Yuri Andropov, another elderly and ill politician, who died in early 1984 after being in office only fifteen months. After Andropov came Konstantin Chernenko, even older and sicker than his predecessor. He survived only thirteen months, until March 1985. As one member of the Soviet old guard succeeded another, President Reagan watched from afar. Neither he nor his tottering counterparts in Moscow saw any point in face-to-face discussions. Ronald Reagan thus became the first American president since Stalin's death to spend a term in office without meeting a Soviet leader.

## RONALD REAGAN AND AMERICAN POWER

Reagan and many of his supporters were convinced that the United States had not done enough to maintain its military strength during the Soviet buildup of the 1960s and 1970s. His administration therefore began the largest

2. Quoted in John Lewis Gaddis, *Russia, the Soviet Union, and the United States: An Interpretive History*, 2d ed. (New York: McGraw-Hill, 1990), p. 318.

3. *The New York Times*, April 15, 1984.

peacetime military buildup in American history. Reagan expanded the Navy to six hundred ships; built a new long-range bomber called the B-1, which President Carter had canceled; and spent billions of dollars for new weapons and additional training to improve ground troops. Critics argued that Reagan's military program was wasteful and creating dangerous federal budget deficits that threatened America's overall economic health. But Reagan was undeterred, and during his first five years in office he spent one third more on defense than President Carter had planned, a grand total of $1.6 *trillion*.

Reagan's concern about growing Soviet military power was shared in part by leaders of America's major NATO allies. They especially feared the hundreds of new SS-20 intermediate-range nuclear missiles the Soviets had begun installing in 1977. To counter those missiles, in 1979 President Carter had agreed to install new and highly accurate American intermediate-range missiles in Western Europe. When the time came to actually install the missiles, the Soviet Union put intense pressure on America's European allies not to accept them. There also were large anti-nuclear demonstrations by European peace activists in several NATO countries. However, in the end both the Reagan and the Western European leaders held firm. Beginning in 1983 the new missiles were installed, but only at the price of further chilling relations with the Soviets.

At about the same time, President Reagan announced a new arms program—this one for defense—called the Strategic Defense Initiative (SDI). The idea was to use powerful space-based lasers and other weapons based on new and unproven technology to shield the United States from hostile nuclear missiles. Many distinguished American scientists argued against the idea—which critics called "Star Wars"—because they were convinced it could not work. On top of that, SDI would be fantastically expensive, and critics feared its enormous costs would further drain

America's economic and scientific resources, which were needed for civilian purposes. The Soviets also strenuously opposed SDI, mainly because they feared yet another costly addition to the arms race based on new technologies in which they trailed the United States. Undeterred by any of the criticism at home or abroad, the Reagan administration began research on what it hoped would provide the United States with the ultimate protection against nuclear missiles.

On September 1, 1983, not long after the SDI program was announced, the Soviet Union shot down a South Korean passenger airliner that had strayed over its territory. All 269 people aboard, including a U.S. congressman, were killed. The Soviets apparently thought the airliner was a U.S. military spy plane. Since they had been tracking the plane over their territory for several hours before shooting it down, this blunder raised grave doubts about Soviet air defense technology and skills. Whatever the reasons for the incident, it sent Soviet-American relations to one of its lowest points since Stalin's death. The official statements by both sides immediately after the crash showed how bad things had become. The United States asked some bitter questions about the Soviet Union:

> *What can we think of a regime that so broadly trumpets its vision of peace and global disarmament and yet so callously and quickly commits a terrorist act to sacrifice the life of innocent human beings? What can be said about Soviet credibility when they so flagrantly lie about such a heinous act? What can be the scope of mutual disclosures with a state whose values permit it to commit such atrocities?*[4]

4. Quoted in Seymour Hersh, *The Target Is Destroyed* (New York: Random House, 1986), p. 130.

The Soviet response, which included the accusation the United States had deliberately provoked the tragedy, was equally angry: "If anyone had any illusion concerning the possibility of an evolution for the better in the policy of the current Administration, events of recent times have thoroughly dispelled them."[5]

As if these disputes were not enough, there were other serious Soviet-American friction points during Reagan's first term as president. Some of them grew out of what was called the Reagan Doctrine, a policy of trying to undermine Marxist regimes in the third world. One policy under the Reagan Doctrine was to send arms and other assistance to rebels in Afghanistan fighting Soviet occupation troops. United States aid helped the Afghans to tie down 100,000 Soviet troops in a hit-and-run war that began to cost the Soviets dearly in lives and money. Despite brutal tactics that included the massacre of civilians, the Soviet army was stalemated.

Soviet and American policies also clashed in Latin America. In October 1983 Reagan sent marines and other troops to overthrow a radical Marxist regime in Grenada, a tiny island in the Caribbean. Whereas that lightning operation took only a few days, the Reagan administration had far greater difficulties in Nicaragua. In 1979 a Marxist-dominated group called the Sandinistas had seized power in Nicaragua, overthrowing a corrupt conservative but pro-American dictatorship. Although President Carter originally had provided the Sandinista regime with some aid, U.S.-Nicaraguan relations deteriorated as the Sandinistas became increasingly dictatorial and allied themselves to both Cuba and the Soviet Union.

Soviet and Cuban support for the Sandinistas infuriated the Reagan administration. In response, the United States armed anti-Sandinista forces known as the contras.

5. *Current Digest of the Soviet Press* 35 (October 26, 1983), p. 1.

Many Americans opposed the policy, but when Congress banned military help to the contras for two years the Reagan administration continued to send it anyway, thereby violating the law and eventually causing a scandal that weakened Reagan's presidency. Meanwhile, the Sandinistas sent aid to pro-Communist rebels in neighboring El Salvador, where another conservative and corrupt regime enjoyed U.S. support.

Despite continued military and economic pressure, Reagan was never able to bring down the Sandinistas. However, in 1990 international pressure forced the Sandinistas to agree to a free election. Their defeat in that election ended their rule in Nicaragua.

Another Soviet-American sore point during the Reagan years was Poland, the country over which the Cold War began back in 1945. In 1980 a weakened Polish regime had been forced by a massive strike to grant Polish workers the first independent trade union in the history of the Communist bloc. But in December of 1981 the union, Solidarity, was crushed when the Soviet-backed regime declared martial law and arrested the union's leadership. This outraged people and governments everywhere in the West.

Meanwhile, as relations with the United States soured during 1983 and 1984, the Soviet Union walked out of three different sets of arms negotiations: talks on reducing long-range nuclear weapons, intermediate-range nuclear

---

**Poles demonstrate in support of the independent labor union Solidarity. In the 1980s the Polish government, like Communist regimes around the world, came under increasing pressure.**

missiles, and conventional forces in Europe. This meant that for the first time in twenty years the two superpowers were not even discussing how to stop the arms race. The so-called new Cold War seemed to be frozen solidly in place. But 1985 was about to dawn, and with the new year came a new warming season in international affairs.

## MIKHAIL GORBACHEV AND
## THE NEW SOVIET FOREIGN POLICY

Mikhail Gorbachev came to power in March of 1985 determined to reform the Soviet system. The Soviet Union was plagued with serious economic, social, and political problems that were many decades old and growing worse because little or nothing had been done to solve them. The country's highly centralized socialist economy was inefficient and riddled with corruption. As a result, the Soviet standard of living was much lower than in the West, and the gap was growing. Serious social problems, such as widespread alcoholism, undermined the health and morale of the people. Although the population was not terrorized by the regime as in Stalin's day, the Soviet Union still was a one-party dictatorship. As a result, millions of Soviet citizens, including many of its best-educated people, felt they had no role in the life of the country as a whole. These people looked for ways to get around the restrictions the state imposed on their lives, rather than getting involved in government-sponsored programs they knew would do the country little or no good.

Gorbachev faced many problems in reforming the So-viet system under a policy he called "perestroika," the Russian word for restructuring. One of the most important involved foreign policy. In order to have the resources to rebuild his country's economy, he had to decrease the huge amount the Soviet Union spent on its military. This meant

Gorbachev had to reduce tensions with the United States. Improved Soviet-American relations would lead to nuclear arms control agreements, which would stop the development of expensive new weapons the Soviet Union could not afford. Beyond that, a less threatening international environment would enable Gorbachev to justify cuts in Soviet ground, naval, and air forces, and transfer the funds saved to civilian needs.

All of this was crucial to Gorbachev because the Soviet Union, with a much smaller economy than the United States, spent as much or more on its military than did the United States. While the United States devoted about six percent of what it produced each year to the military, in the Soviet Union the military claimed about twenty-five percent of annual production. This included the labor of the country's best scientists and engineers and the products of its best factories. It was a situation that had existed since Stalin's time, and one that Gorbachev knew he had to end if his country were to solve its problems and prosper. Hardly less important, improved Soviet-American relations and arms control would make both countries more secure. They would then be free to cooperate on serious global problems, such as damage to the environment, that threatened all nations.

Gorbachev wasted no time in breaking with the past policies that had soured relations with the United States. To his credit, President Reagan responded positively, and the dark gloom of the late 1970s and early 1980s quickly began to lift. Five months after coming into office, Gorbachev announced the Soviet Union was suspending its nuclear weapons tests. He then traveled to Paris, where he was a huge public relations success as the beginning of what would be called "Gorby fever" began to sweep Western Europe. In November, Gorbachev and Reagan came to Geneva, Switzerland, for their first meeting. Although that meeting did not produce any concrete results, it was warm and friendly. The smiles and handshakes the two leaders exchanged in Geneva were a sharp and welcome contrast to the coldness that had kept Reagan from meeting with Brezhnev, Andropov, and Chernenko.

The first Reagan-Gorbachev attempt to negotiate an arms control treaty came at a hurriedly and poorly prepared summit meeting in Reykjavík, Iceland, in October 1986. The meeting failed because Reagan refused to accept Gorbachev's demand that the United States abandon its SDI ("Star Wars") program. Once again, Soviet and American leaders faced each other grimly as the meeting ended. However, both sides were determined to overcome the setback. Barely a year later, in December 1987, Gorbachev came to Washington to sign a U.S.-Soviet treaty that eliminated all intermediate-range nuclear missiles the two powers had in Europe. In terms of absolute numbers, the 1987 agreement was a minor treaty. It eliminated only four percent of each side's nuclear arsenal. But in terms of the Cold War and the nuclear arms race, it was a giant step. For the first time ever in the Cold War, both sides had *reduced* their nuclear arsenals and eliminated an entire category of nuclear arms.

The Cold War thawed further in February 1988 when Gorbachev announced that the Soviet Union would withdraw its troops from Afghanistan within a year. The announcement was greeted with skepticism, but on February 15, 1989, the last Soviet soldier departed from Afghanistan. Meanwhile, Gorbachev had come to New York to speak to the United Nations General Assembly. During the speech Gorbachev pledged that the Soviet Union would reduce its huge army by 500,000 men and 10,000 tanks. More important, however, were his remarks about the use of force in general:

*It is obvious . . . that the use or threat of force no longer can or must be an instrument of foreign*

Mikhail Gorbachev reversed Soviet foreign policy,
rejecting the idea of Communist-capitalist struggle.

*policy. This applies above all to nuclear arms, but that is not the only thing that matters. All of us, and primarily the stronger of us, must exercise self-restraint and totally rule out any outward-oriented use of force.*[6]

In effect, in barely three years Gorbachev had abandoned the main principles of Soviet foreign policy. Since the founding of the Soviet Union, its leaders had assumed that they were in a battle to the death with the capitalist world. Lenin and Stalin had believed the issue would be settled by war. Nikita Khrushchev, living under the shadow of nuclear arms, had rejected that idea as suicidal. He had announced the doctrine of "peaceful coexistence." But even that doctrine assumed an economic and political competition in which communism—by providing a higher standard of living for its people—would defeat and eliminate capitalism. Gorbachev went much further than Khrushchev's "peaceful coexistence" doctrine. He rejected the Communist-capitalist struggle. The two systems would simply live side by side, with people under each system ordering their lives as they saw fit.

---

## REVOLUTION IN EASTERN EUROPE AND THE END OF THE COLD WAR

---

By 1989 the Cold War had faded to little more than an annoying chill. But it was not entirely over. For over four decades the Soviets maintained a tight but uneasy grip on Eastern Europe, as their military might kept corrupt, inefficient, and unpopular Communist governments in power. However, it cost the Soviets huge amounts of money to maintain troops in Eastern Europe. Propping up the ineffi-

6. *The New York Times*, December 8, 1988.

cient Eastern European economies cost even more. Added to that was the immense expense of the Cold War that Soviet control of Eastern Europe had provoked.

By 1989 those burdens had become too heavy to bear. Meanwhile, as reform swept the Soviet Union after 1985, pressure increased on the Eastern European Communist regimes to change as well. Because these regimes were so unpopular, their leaders hesitated, and the governments became shakier with each passing day. During 1989 Gorbachev himself warned the Communist leaders in Eastern Europe that they must introduce reforms or risk being swept away. But his warning came far too late. In April the entire rotten structure of Eastern European communism began to buckle.

The collapse started in Poland, where the government, desperate to win some public support, agreed to allow the Solidarity trade union to reorganize and participate in free elections. Solidarity won an overwhelming victory in June, and by August Poland had its first non-Communist government in over forty years. The crash of communism in Poland began a chain reaction that swept across the rest of the region. Hungary's government fell in October. That same month Erich Honecker, the hard-line Communist leader of East Germany, was removed from office. In a last-ditch effort to survive, on November 9 his successors opened the Berlin Wall. For the first time in twenty-eight years, East Germans could freely cross over to West Berlin. Suddenly the Berlin Wall, for so long a place of defeat, despair, and death, was overwhelmed by the shouting, singing, and stomping of celebrating people. *The New York Times* described the scene:

*By 1 A.M., celebrating Berliners, East and West . . .*
*[were] blowing on trumpets, dancing, laughing,*
*and absorbing a glittering scene. . . . East Berliners*
*said cars were backed up for more than a mile on*

**Berliners walk on the infamous Wall on November 10, 1989, the day after the border between their city's eastern and western sectors was finally opened.**

*the eastern side of some border crossings, as East Berliners abandoned their cars for a quick taste of the West on foot.*[7]

Since 1961 the Wall had been the symbol of the Cold War; in 1989 its fate symbolized the end of the Cold War.

The Bulgarian regime fell the next day. By December, Czechoslovakia had a non-Communist government and the Communist dictator of Romania had been overthrown. After forty-five years, Communism and Soviet control over Eastern Europe were dead. All that remained was to bury the Cold War itself.

The crucial person in this historic development was Mikhail Gorbachev. The Soviet leader, to be sure, wanted the Communist regimes in Eastern Europe to reform, not fall. However, once the collapse began, the Soviet leader did nothing to stop it. Saving communism in Eastern Europe would have required great bloodshed and the continuation of the Cold War. It also would have meant the end of Gorbachev's reform program in the Soviet Union. So Gorbachev sacrificed Eastern Europe to continue his reforms at home, end the Cold War, and establish normal peaceful relations with the United States and its allies.

The official end of the Cold War came in 1990. At a summit meeting in June, Gorbachev and George Bush, the new American president, signed agreements dealing with both chemical and nuclear weapons. The next month Gorbachev agreed to German reunification, dropping a long-standing Soviet demand that a reunified Germany not be a member of NATO. Accepting German unification was a difficult decision for Gorbachev, as it was in many ways for the United States, Great Britain, and France. Neither the Soviet Union nor the West had forgotten the horrors Ger-

7. *The New York Times*, November 19, 1989.

many had unleashed upon the world during World War II. However, immense German pressure on both the Western powers and the Soviet Union led them to give way. While all nations received promises about Germany's peaceful intentions, the Soviet Union in addition received billions of dollars in German aid it desperately needed. Germany's official reunification took place on October 3, erasing yet another mark of the Cold War. Twelve days later Mikhail Gorbachev was awarded the Nobel Peace Prize for 1990, an honor he richly deserved.

On November 17, 1990, the United States, the Soviet Union, and thirty other nations signed the Paris Charter, which officially ended the Cold War. The finale of this long, bitter, and costly struggle came quietly. After signing the charter, President Bush spoke for a happy but tired world when he said, without fanfare: "We have closed a chapter in history. The Cold War is over."[8]

## THE COLD WAR IN RETROSPECT

On one level there were some clear winners in the Cold War. The struggle was settled on American terms. The Soviet Union left Eastern Europe and abandoned its old ambition of promoting Communist revolutions worldwide. Moreover, within thirteen months of the Cold War's official end, the Soviet Union itself disintegrated. In place of the former Communist giant were fifteen independent states, all of which rejected communism.

On a deeper level, the results of the Cold War represented a victory for freedom and democracy over totalitarian dictatorship. In 1945 not only was the Soviet Union taking control of Eastern Europe, but communism and

8. Quoted in William G. Hyland, *The Cold War: Fifty Years of Conflict* (New York: Times Books, 1991), p. 199.

dictatorship cast a dark shadow over troubled Western Europe, where in the wreckage of World War II the survival of democracy was in doubt. Beginning with the Truman Doctrine and the Marshall Plan, the United States contained the expansion of Soviet power and helped the democratic states of Western Europe to recover their strength. Thereafter, despite many mistakes and questionable policies, the United States on balance provided crucial support for advocates of freedom on both sides of the Iron Curtain. American power and the success of its democratic political system and free enterprise economy also were essential in forcing the Soviet leadership, finally, to undertake reforms. Those reforms not only ended the Cold War but destroyed Communist totalitarianism.

At the same time the Cold War had many losers besides the Soviet Union. For forty-five years the Cold War struggle consumed much of the energy and strength of the United States. Too often American leaders viewed international problems through the prism of the Cold War, rather than looking at local conditions. This led to support for repressive regimes that trumpeted their "anti-Communism" while mistreating their poverty-stricken citizens. It also led to intervention against governments that were considered too friendly to the Soviet Union but in fact were no threat to American interests. These actions not only tarnished the United States' image around the world but in the long run undermined the welfare of its citizens at home.

In addition, the Cold War led the United States to pour resources into the military that were needed for civilian purposes. America's cities, schools, health care, and transportation network deteriorated while its national debt grew, in part as a price for waging the Cold War. This overemphasis on the military undermined the competitiveness of America's civilian economy. That in part explains why Germany and especially Japan, which focused mainly on producing consumer goods, have taken many markets from American industries, including markets in the United States itself. In fact, some observers have remarked that it was Germany and Japan, the losers of World War II, who "won" the Cold War.

At the same time, it is already clear that many parts of the post–Cold War world will be less safe and more violent than they were during the Cold War. In the Middle East a major conflict erupted the same year the Cold War ended when Iraq invaded Kuwait. That crisis lasted until 1991, when a coalition of nations led by the United States used military force to drive the Iraqis out of their small oil-rich neighbor. Yet Iraq's defeat only strengthened neighboring Iran, which was financing extremist Islamic fundamentalist groups that threatened Arab regimes throughout the region. In Eastern Europe and Central Asia, where Communist dictatorships once kept ethnic strife under control, long-smoldering hatreds have flared up into several civil wars. In Africa ethnic conflict and economic chaos have produced warfare and widespread suffering. Meanwhile, aggressive regimes in Iraq, Iran, Libya, and North Korea are seeking either to buy or build nuclear weapons.

Clearly, coping with these problems will require international cooperation. During the early 1990s a model for achieving just that seemed to be developing, based on the United Nations. The U.S.-led coalition that drove Iraq out of Kuwait did so on the basis of UN resolutions. In the East African nation of Somalia, torn by civil war, soldiers from several nations acting under UN authority brought food and supplies to starving people. In the former Yugoslavia, which split into several parts as the Cold War ended, soldiers wearing blue United Nations helmets struggled to stop bitter warfare between ethnic groups.

It seemed clear that the post–Cold War world would have only one superpower: the United States. But while the military power of the United States was unequaled, its economic strength compared with other countries had been greatly reduced. Faced with serious problems at home, and lacking the resources to solve many of them, the United States had far less to spare for activities overseas. Thus its world role seemed likely to be less dominant than it was between 1945 and 1990.

Nonetheless, every time the United Nations has acted effectively since the end of the Cold War, United States leadership has been essential. So it is likely that the old Cold War rivalry—the United States versus the Soviet Union—will be replaced by a new post–Cold War partnership: the United States and the United Nations. That combination's success or failure will do a lot to determine how well the world will solve the problems the Cold War left behind.

# FOR FURTHER READING

Ambrose, Stephen E. *Rise to Globalism: American Foreign Policy Since 1938*, 6th rev. ed. New York: Penguin Books, 1991.

Brzezinski, Zbigniew. *The Grand Failure: The Birth and Death of Communism in the Twentieth Century.* New York: Collier Books, 1990.

Divine, Robert A. *Since 1945: Politics and Diplomacy in Recent American History*, 3d ed. New York: Knopf, 1985.

Gaddis, John Lewis. *Russia, the Soviet Union, and the United States: An Interpretive History*, 2d ed. New York, McGraw-Hill, 1990.

———. *Strategies of Containment.* New York: Oxford University Press, 1982.

Gillon, Steven, and Diane B. Kunz, eds. *America During the Cold War.* Fort Worth: Harcourt Brace Jovanovich, 1993.

Hogan, Michael J., ed. *The End of the Cold War.* New York: Cambridge University Press, 1992.

Hyland, William G. *The Cold War: Fifty Years of Conflict.* New York: Times Books, 1991.

Levering, Ralph B. *The Cold War, 1945–1987*, 2d ed. Arlington Heights: Harlan Davidson, 1987.

Weisberger, Bernard A. *Cold War, Cold Peace: The United States and Russia Since 1945.* New York: American Heritage, 1984.

# INDEX

Khrushchev, Nikita, 64, 70, 72, 73, 75, 79, 82–83, 88, *93*, 94–96, 98, 101–104, 115, 148
Kim Il-Sung, 50, 51
Kissinger, Henry, 15, 120, 127
Korean War, 16, 49–53, *54*, 55, *56*, 57–58, 62, 74
Kosygin, Alexei, *116*, 117
Kuwait, 154

Laos, 114
Lebanon, 79
Lenin, Vladimir, 21, *22*, 148
Libya, 154

MacArthur, Douglas, 53, 55, 57
Malenkov, Georgi, 70
Mao Zedong, 57, 78, 127
Marshall, George C., 40–41, 66
Marshall Plan, 40–41, *42*, 43, 153
Massive retaliation, 71
McCarren, Pat, 66
McCarthy, Joseph, 66, *67*, 68
McNamara, Robert, 102
Morganthau, Hans, 14
Mossadegh, Mohammed, 80
Mozambique, 16
Multiple independently targeted reentry vehicle (MIRV), 122, 126
Munich agreement, 23, 26

Napoleon I, Emperor, 19
Nasser, Gamal Abdel, 76, 78–79
Nazi-Soviet pact, 23
Nicaragua, 16, 115, 141–142
Nixon, Richard M., 112, 115, 118, 120–121, 123, 124, 127, *128*, 129–131
North Atlantic Treaty Organization (NATO), 46, 48, 78, 120, 139, 151

North Korea, 154 (*see also* Korean War)
North Vietnam (*see* Vietnam; Vietnam War)
Nuclear Nonproliferation Treaty (1968), 124
Nuclear test ban treaty (1963), 124
Nuclear weapons, 12, 14, 48, 71, 73, 81–82, 88, 95–98, *99*, 100–104, 117–118, 121–122, 124, *125*, 126, 142, 144–146, 151, 154

Operation Mongoose, 94

Panmunjom, 55
Paris Charter, 152
Peace Corps, 88
Peaceful coexistence, 71, 73, 148
People's Republic of China, 51, 52, 57–58, 74, 95, 104, 108, 112, 120, 126–127, *128*, 129
Perestroika, 144
Peterson, Peter G., 124
Poland, 28, 29, 32, 34, 123, 142, *143*, 149
Potsdam Conference, 33

Reagan, Ronald, 135, *136*, 137–139, 141, 142, 145, 146
Reagan Doctrine, 141
Rhee, Syngman, 50, 51, 71
Romania, 29, 32, 151
Roosevelt, Franklin D., 25, 26, 27, 28–30
Russo-Japanese War, 49

SALT (Strategic Arms Limitation Talks), 118, 123
SALT I, 124, 126
SALT II, 134
Sandinistas, 141–142